The "Hidden" Project Drivers

The "Hidden" Project Drivers

Building Behavior that Drives Success

Kursten Faller and
Alan Weiss

BUSINESS EXPERT PRESS
Leader in applied, concise business books

First published in 2026 by
Business Expert Press, LLC
222 East 46th Street, New York, NY 10017
www.businessexpertpress.com

ISBN-13: 978-1-63742-954-9 (paperback)
ISBN-13: 978-1-63742-955-6 (e-book)

Business Expert Press Portfolio and Project Management Collection

First edition: 2026

10 9 8 7 6 5 4 3 2 1

EU SAFETY REPRESENTATIVE
Mare Nostrum Group B.V.
Doelen 72
4831 GR Breda
The Netherlands
gpsr@mare-nostrum.co.uk

For Marie, my daughter, whose growth inspires my own. May these lessons offer light on your path.

Description

Projects do not fail because the plan was wrong. They fail because the people running the plan were not led with clarity, courage, and care. *The Hidden Project Drivers* **shows why charts and status meetings are not enough in a world defined by speed and uncertainty, and it replaces control with leadership rooted in behavioral science and neuroscience.**

You will learn how to create psychological safety so ideas surface early, convert compliance into ownership so teams move on their own energy, make cleaner decisions at higher velocity, and turn healthy tension into a crucible for innovation. Through vivid stories, practical exercises, and the Project Pulse highlights that anchor each chapter, you will shift your mental models, update your maps, and build environments where people think better together.

Artificial intelligence can draft plans and schedule meetings. It cannot build trust, resolve friction, or inspire commitment. That is your job as a leader. This book gives you the tools and language to do it with confidence.

This is not a manual for administration. It is a field guide for leaders who want to deliver results while growing people. If you lead projects, portfolios, or transformations, **this book will help you move faster, reduce waste, and unlock the human factors that actually drive success.**

Contents

List of Figures

Acknowledgements

I owe a deep debt of gratitude to my mentor, Ron Dedman, who recognized potential in me long before I could see it myself. I will never forget the day he looked across his desk and said, "You are a teacher." Only now do I truly understand those words. Ron has been a steady presence throughout my journey, and it was during one of our conversations that he encouraged me to write this book. His belief in me made all the difference.

I am thankful to my publisher, BEP, for the opportunity to share these ideas more widely. I am also grateful to my first coach, Jasmine Kernaleguen, who helped me bring order to the chaos and begin a transformation that shaped my path. My thanks go as well to Alan Weiss, whose insights and encouragement challenged me to think more boldly and sustained me through the writing process.

To my wife, Andie, I give my deepest thanks for creating the space for me to pursue my dreams with unwavering support and love. Your encouragement has carried me through every stage of this work.

Introduction

Project management isn't just a skillset; it's a shift in mindset. You can't lead modern projects with yesterday's thinking, no matter how many new tools you stack on top. If you're picturing Gantt charts, risk logs, and long-winded status updates with too many acronyms, then you're still managing as if it's the 1960s. And if that's your toolkit, you're already on the path to extinction. The meteor's about to hit, and most folks just haven't looked up yet.

Most project managers I've met (my younger self included) come from technical backgrounds, such as engineers, IT folks, analysts, you name it. That was my path too. Early in my leadership career, I genuinely thought project management was about control, about building the perfect plan and then trying to force people to follow it.

Spoiler alert: that didn't work.

I didn't realize it at the time, *but I was the problem.* Not the team. Not the tools, me. I didn't know any different, and no one around me really did either. Most of us were just repeating what we'd seen. "Best practices," they called it.

The truth? I've met very few people who actually get what it means to lead a project well, not herd it, not monitor it, but lead it. *It's an art form, not a spreadsheet.*

One of my first mentors described it like this: Being a project manager is like being the conductor of an orchestra. You don't play every instrument; you bring the chaos into harmony and create a symphony. He also told me, "You can take a horse to water, but you can't make it *think*." That one stuck with me too and saved me from a lot of unnecessary stress.

And yet, like most students of the game, I kept going down the rabbit hole of rote learning. More books. More certifications. More frameworks.

Eventually, though, something cracked open. I started finding tools and ways of thinking that weren't just about controlling chaos; they were about understanding it. I started seeing the matrix for what it was: lines of code, stories, and behaviors. Once you can see it, you can bend the rules. Not in a manipulative way, more like finding the gaps where real leadership actually lives.

The old ways don't hold up anymore. The world's too complex, too fast. We can't rely on 5-year roadmaps and rigid processes when everything around us is shifting weekly. We're in a different game now, and it demands a different kind of project leader.

The future of project management is grounded in behavioral science and neuroscience. It's about influence, emotion, clarity, and conflict. And the raw materials don't just live in projects; they show up in every relationship, in every team, at work and at home.

Here's the kicker: AI is already doing the human–computer stuff. It can build your project plans, balance your budgets, and schedule your meetings. But what it can't do, not yet and probably not for a long time, is lead people. Inspire them. Hold space for tension. Resolve the invisible friction and tough work through it.

That's the work that matters now.

So if you're still clinging to the old playbook, waiting for a return to the "way things were," you're already behind. You don't have to like that, but you probably need to hear it.

This book is for the ones ready to evolve. To lead in the turmoil. To listen harder. To influence without controlling. And to finally let go of the illusion that being a great project manager is about being the smartest person in the room.

It's not.

Let's go.

—Kursten Faller and Alan Weiss
June 6, 2026

CHAPTER 1

The Engine of Change: Projects Drive Everything that Moves and Matters

Projects are essential in today's world of constant change. Think "big" to realize that projects aren't about creating things for the sake of creating things; they need to provide value. That incremental value allows organizations to achieve their strategy. Without people also changing, whatever technology, products, or processes that may be created can't reach their potential.

Welcome to the Age of Permanent Disruption

The "Old Normal" was already shifting, and there is no "new normal" or "return to normal." Instead, there is No Normal®. After all, "normal" means "average" or "typical," and who wants to be average and typical?

The world is reorganizing, digitally, economically, and socially. These are synergistic forces at work, even though they often seem "at odds" with each other. It's not our contention that artificial intelligence (AI) will take over the world or that everything around us is crumbling (the Chicken Little school of philosophy). But it's apparent that many existing jobs will be lost, new jobs created, and many jobs altered. Commensurately, jobs, income, and status will change.

Once upon a time, paper companies ran three shifts of 20 people each on each machine. It was better to lose money on lowered prices than to shut down the machines. The machines had a "wet end" and a "dry end." Today, two people run the machines each shift, one up in the booth with a keyboard and one on the floor with a screwdriver! (There is an old story of a man and a dog being the sole people who show up at a factory in the morning and leave in the evening. When someone inquired about the strange arrangement, they were told that the dog was there to ensure the man didn't touch anything, and the man was there to feed the dog.)

"Disruption" and "volatility" were conditions we tolerated (although they would constitute a great name for a law firm), while we awaited the return to that "normal" and historical life. But consider these seismic facts:

1. Until recent times, since about 1993, the "Boomer" and subsequent Gen X constituted the preponderance of corporate, nonprofit, academic, and political leadership. That cohort has now largely departed, and now Millennials and Gen Z have moved into those positions, with vastly different frames of reference.

Project Pulse

Disruption and volatility are opportunities for growth and competitive edge, not dangers to be defended against.

---

2. In current times, the largest intergenerational transfer of wealth ever is taking place due to the original U.S., Reagan-era creation of IRA, SEP IRA, and 401K legislation.

We can name far more substantial economic and societal changes, but you can readily see them all around us.

One of those changes is in climate, where winter doesn't "usher in" spring anymore, but rather leads to uncertain conditions. It can be 65° in December in northern latitudes and 45° in the spring. What we've taken for granted now must be examined more closely, and nowhere is that truer than in business. "Business as usual" means little when there is no "usual"!

One further and obvious example: COVID was an accelerator of required change that left permanent transformation, from take-out and delivered meals, to declines in business travel and increases in tourist travel. Our faith in certain sources has been diminished, particularly in the media, and in politics.

Thus, we have new generations "at the controls" that lack institutional memory and are still trying to figure out what would seem like basic issues, for example, how do you manage remote and hybrid workers, or how do you find talent in a declining population, or how do we control AI best for our purposes.

"Credentials" are giving way to competence: "shop" classes are being very successfully reintroduced in high schools so that college is not a mandatory option upon graduation, and airlines are no longer requiring that pilots have college educations, on the intelligent assumption that it's much more important to know how to land a plane than it is to discuss Schopenhauer with the passengers.

If that's the past and present, then let's take a brief look at the future.

Strategy Succeeds or Fails Because of Projects

Jeff Bezos has consistently demonstrated an unusually candid view of Amazon's future, acknowledging that even the most powerful companies are not immune to decline. In a 2018 all-hands meeting with employees, Bezos starkly stated: "Amazon is not too big to fail...in fact, I predict one day Amazon will fail. Amazon will go bankrupt." He went on to say that the company's job was to "delay that day as long as possible."[1]

For Bezos, this isn't fatalism, it's strategic realism. He has long argued that the primary threat to Amazon isn't external competitors, but internal decay. He warns that "If we start to focus on ourselves, instead of focusing on our customers, that will be the beginning of the end." This echoes a core Bezos principle repeated in many of his shareholder letters: customer obsession is not just a differentiator; it's a survival imperative.

In his 2016 letter to shareholders, Bezos wrote: "Day 2 is stasis. Followed by irrelevance. Followed by excruciating, painful decline. Followed by death. And that is why it is always Day 1." (Amazon Shareholder Letter, 2016). This "Day 1" philosophy reflects his belief that companies must continually operate with the urgency and focus of a startup, no matter how large they become.

---

[1] CNBC Article November 15, 2018.

Bezos has also referenced the typical lifespan of large corporations to illustrate his point: "Most companies that are of our size are well along the way to going out of business." Rather than celebrate Amazon's scale, he sees it as a vulnerability unless consciously defended against the forces of stagnation.

In sum, Bezos sees Amazon's death not as an "if," but a "when." His focus is on elongating the arc of the company's relevance through a relentless commitment to innovation, operational excellence, and above all, listening to customers. For him, leadership means acknowledging impermanence and acting every day to fight it.

There is a book called *Smaller, Faster, Lighter, Denser, Cheaper*[2] wherein the author points to the inevitable movement toward these goals. And that was before AI began to seriously influence the landscape. This is why we talk of "better" practices and not "best" practices, because one should always be getting better and never imagine they are the "best," which leads to complacency. It's too simple to achieve "full speed ahead" but for the wrong destination.

Project Pulse

Comedian Bob Newhart had a routine where, as pilot of a transatlantic flight, he announced to the passengers that they were setting a new speed record crossing the Atlantic, and would be landing an hour ahead of schedule....in either Montreal or Buenos Aires.

Think of projects as the engine room powering the ship.

In Figure 1.1, we see that strategy and leadership without execution means you never leave the dock, never set sail; strategy and execution without leadership means you're adrift without direction; and leadership and execution without strategy means that you have no destination because no wind is a good wind if you don't know your next port of call.

Kodak once dominated the film market; in fact, many people thought that it was a law that all film had to be packed in yellow boxes. Yet Kodak was hiring chemists for its film emulsions right up to the age of digital

---

[2] Robert Bryce, Hachette Book Group, 2014.

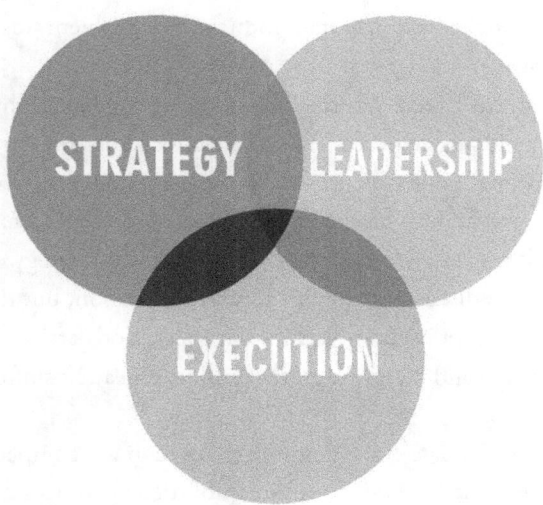

Figure 1.1 Strategy/leadership/execution synergy

photography when it went out of the film business. We can call that "strategy as still life." That's fine for the arts, not so good for business.

Strategy is a destination which is periodically updated, not a fate etched in stone (or emulsion). Yahoo has demonstrated that strategy without leadership is just noise and not a siren call to investors.

The WeWork direction was more mirage and illusion than business strategy. Alan has published a book, *Sentient Strategy*,[3] which advises setting a strategy in a day, looking one year ahead. Looking farther into the future, some firms still try to see 5 or 10 years ahead, and wasting weeks that don't improve the quality of the process is like using a horse-drawn wagon to get to work. Unless you're Amish, it makes no sense in this day and age.

Kodak's fall is not a story of ignorance. It's a story of foresight without follow-through. Contrary to popular myth, Kodak didn't miss the digital revolution; it helped start it. In 1975, one of its own engineers, Steve Sasson, built the world's first digital camera. Leadership recognized the potential early and even invested in digital imaging R&D throughout the 1980s and 1990s. Strategically, Kodak understood that the future of photography was digital. It filed patents, explored digital

---

[3] Taylor and Francis, 2023.

printers, and launched early digital products. The problem wasn't vision; it was execution.

What paralyzed Kodak was the inability to act on its insight with the urgency and boldness required. The company's leadership struggled to resolve a deep internal conflict: How to pursue a digital future without cannibalizing its highly profitable film business. This tension bred hesitation, half-measures, and internal resistance. The strategy existed on paper, and leaders discussed the need for transformation, but the organizational will to disrupt itself was lacking. In effect, Kodak tried to straddle two worlds, analog and digital, until the ground beneath it shifted too fast to keep up.

By the time Kodak fully committed to digital, competitors like Canon and Sony had seized the lead, unburdened by legacy business models. Kodak declared bankruptcy in 2012, not because it lacked a strategy, but because it failed to execute decisively. It's a cautionary tale that strategy and leadership are not enough when courage is absent. The digital future doesn't wait for consensus; it rewards those who act with clarity and conviction.

There Is No Change if People Don't Change

In early 20th-century Germany, a horse named Clever Hans captivated audiences and baffled experts. Hans appeared to possess astonishing intelligence: He could count, perform arithmetic, spell out words, and even respond to questions by tapping his hoof. To onlookers, Hans was not just a trained animal; he seemed to be reasoning, calculating, and even communicating. Scientists, teachers, and journalists flocked to see him, wondering if this horse might redefine the boundaries of animal cognition.

But as psychologist Oskar Pfungst later revealed, Hans wasn't actually solving problems. He was reading subtle, unconscious cues from his human handlers; tiny changes in posture, breath, or facial expressions that signaled when to stop tapping. Hans didn't understand numbers or language. He understood people. His performance mimicked intelligence, but the underlying mechanism was entirely different: conditioned response, not comprehension.

Clever Hans became a cautionary tale not just in the study of animal behavior, but in how we interpret competence. What looks like understanding can often be finely tuned mimicry. The danger isn't just that we're fooled; it's that we build systems, decisions, or leadership credibility on top of that illusion. In teams, organizations, and even individual development, it's easy to confuse surface fluency with depth, responsiveness with reasoning, and appearance with substance. People have to change to perceive change, and to appreciate the fact that old behaviors and beliefs won't produce new initiatives or innovation.

Hans didn't lie, but the narrative around him did. His story reminds us to look beyond performance and ask harder questions about what's really going on beneath the surface. In a world increasingly filled with dashboards, metrics, and performative behaviors, the Clever Hans effect is as relevant today as it was in a dusty Berlin courtyard over a century ago.

Project Pulse

Don't mistake motion for mastery. Real value lies beneath the surface, not in the performance of best practices.

From the Engine Room to the Bridge: A New Kind of Project Manager

Project managers were once engineers in the engine room, but now they have to serve as captains. You don't want to end up in Alaska in January or Key West in August. (A classic movie line by Lorna Dern: "It was as hot as Georgia Asphalt in August—Blue Velvet, 1986.)

This means we have to understand organizational outcomes, or to think about Figure 1.1, strategy and execution but no leadership, no destination. Futures, however, are actually forged in projects. Projects "forge" future leaders, creating accountability, discipline, and properly applied authority. Conversely, future leaders forge successful projects with innovation, energy, and ambition.

The Project Management Institute (PMI) has finally grasped the importance of this reciprocity in their Global Project Management Job Trends 2023 report, they state:

> *To remain competitive, companies will need to focus on hiring problem solvers and relationship builders who can help them drive change and deliver strategic value.*

That sounds like being on the bridge to us. To get there requires "trial by fire," a crucible that can anneal elements in volatile and transformative times, requiring rare earths (foresight, discipline, and collaboration) to create future and sustainable success.

Too many people find and then stop at "data": some proceed to "information"; a few go on to knowledge": and a talented few proceed to "wisdom." Thus, wisdom is a process that is earned after experience and evaluation. No one learns to ride a bike in a class or with a book. It's experiential, and requires some bruised knees and a helmet.

A badge or initials after your name, or memberships and honorifics, will not buy you respect and certainly not success. Best practices become so in hindsight and retrospect, and that's why the constant search for "better practices" leads more assuredly to sustainable success.

CHAPTER 2

Leadership:
The Unseen Edge

Here we explore how values and beliefs drive behavior. Fear disrupts cognition and interrupts behavior that contributes positively to projects. The way to shift behavior is influence beliefs and values. Effective coaching engages cognitive processes to generate insights that lead to reevaluation. All great leaders are actually great coaches, which leads them to be far more effective in achieving objectives with less effort. How can you become a great coach?

Expertise Alone Won't Win the Race

Modern project management was created by NASA in the 1960s, and its antecedents were before that. The vast majority of practitioners come from a technical background trained as engineers, programmers, and other scientific professions. Projects are about people, and you need to lead effectively to be successful, which is a gap for most project managers. Without a focus on the behavior of people and teams, it's impossible to deliver projects successfully.

The Historical Blueprint was NASA and construction roots. Project management's lineage was born in engineering, logistics, and control-heavy environments. The legacy mindset has been planning, scheduling, and reporting. This leads us to "the expertise trap."

Technical backgrounds create blind spots with human dynamics.

Expertise can give a false sense of superiority or control in people-driven systems. Charts and graphs alone are insufficient for considering the human element. After all, traditionally, organizations saw their equipment as assets and people as expenses. That began to change with the human potential movement coming to the fore in the 1960s. That made behavioral sciences the new core.

We can look at today's project leaders as human engineers. Daniel Kahneman was an American-Israeli psychologist who was a co-winner of the 2002 Nobel Prize in Economic Sciences. He focused on the psychology of judgment and decision making in leadership.[1] Amy C. Edmonson of Harvard Business School has focused on psychological safety in teams.

Psychological safety, as defined by Edmondson, is the belief within a team that the environment is safe for interpersonal risk-taking. This means that team members feel comfortable expressing themselves, sharing ideas, asking questions, raising concerns, and admitting mistakes without fear of negative consequences like punishment or humiliation.[2]

Daniel Pink argued that in the new economy, the premium shifts from logic to meaning, from analysis to empathy, and from command-and-control to creativity and connection. He calls this the "*Conceptual Age*," where success depends on the very skills behavioral science helps us understand: how people think, feel, engage, and collaborate.

In this age, project leaders aren't just managers of time and scope; they are *navigators of motivation, trust, and team dynamics*. It's not enough to control the plan; you have to inspire the people executing it. That's why technical fluency alone is no longer enough. Behavioral fluency is now the real competitive edge.

Beyond Gantt Charts: How You Show Up Matters

We have to move "beyond" Gantt Charts to conversations. We tend to create the *illusion of control* by counting, comparing, charting, and analyzing. But this is too often illusory, like the executive team perusing a fishbone diagram on an operator's machine while ignoring the oil leaking around their shoes. What delays projects, plans, and purpose more than anything in interpersonal friction, whether accidental (unshared information) or deliberate (withheld information).

---

[1] *Thinking Fast and Slow,* Farrar, Straus and Giroux, 2011.
[2] *The Fearless Organization,* Wiley, 2018.

After World War II, American leadership faced a choice: trust in the power of its ideals, democracy, and liberty, self-determination, or intervene directly to force outcomes abroad. Too often, it chose the latter. The result was paradoxical: efforts to ***control global affairs often undermined the very values they were meant to protect***.

The same pattern plays out in organizations. Leaders who don't trust the culture, values, or shared purpose of their teams often reach for tools of control, rigid plans, tight supervision, and imposed decisions. Just like foreign interventions, these actions tend to backfire. They create dependency, erode trust, and suppress initiative.

Project leadership in today's world requires ***a different kind of confidence***: not in your ability to control everything, but in the system you've nurtured: the values you've lived, the culture you've shaped, and the people you've empowered.

We've all seen "The Iceberg," where visible behaviors are only a tiny aspect of the attitudes and beliefs supporting the small portion we can see.

Project Pulse

Effective leaders create and shape what isn't otherwise readily seen.

"Culture" is that set of beliefs that governs behavior. It sets the expectations and standards for when "no one else is in the room" or, if they are, no one is watching.

Vignette: Resort Culture

From a high balcony at a beach resort at about 6 a.m., I was watching the employee in the tractor clearing the beach and smoothing the sand. He had no idea I was watching him. When he passed some trash that had blown into an alley next to the hotel, he stopped the machine and walked 25 yards over and back to collect what the machine would have missed.

On another occasion, I watched two hotel executives in suits and ties walking through the pool area on a 90+ day. One turned to his right and walked 10 yards to pick up a candy wrapper on the ground and deposit it in the trash another few yards away. Then they both resumed their walk.

Figure 2.1 The illusory Iceberg

Think of this like an iceberg as shown in Figure 2.1 below. The behavior is the tip of the iceberg you see above the surface. The beliefs and attitudes that drive the behavior are what's hidden below.

Wouldn't we all be delighted to know that even when unwatched, employees were "doing the right thing," setting examples for their peers and even the members, guests, customers, and clients?

No one in organizations really believes what they read or hear; they only truly believe what they see. Hence, leaders are the avatars, and should be demonstrating "above the water line" what's below. What's called "psychological safety" is about creating trust that enables the desired performance. Projects don't fail from poor planning or formulation, but mostly from poor implementation that is the result of a lack of trust, of fear of being "whacked" (criticized, punished, and made the scapegoat in the hunt for blame instead of the cause of problems and delays).

Vignette: The PM Who Let Go

Sophie was a senior project manager brought in to turn around a failing digital transformation initiative. The sponsor wanted "tighter controls," more detailed reporting, and stricter approval gates. The previous PM had already implemented weekly dashboards, daily standups, and a three-layered risk register, and yet the project was still behind, and morale was sinking.

Instead of doubling down on control, Sophie did something different. She stopped managing the plan and started leading the people.

She sat down with each team member and asked one question: *"What's slowing you down?"* The answers weren't about scope or risk logs, they were about fear, unclear priorities, and not feeling heard.

She stripped away layers of reporting, gave teams the freedom to experiment, and had real conversations with stakeholders about trade-offs. She **trusted the team to act like adults**, and in return, they started acting like owners.

Six weeks later, the project was back on track not because she tight-***ened the reins, but because she let go of the illusion of control and focused on creating alignment and trust***.

Control is seductive, and it feels safe. However, in complex systems, control often slows progress. What moves projects forward isn't more process; it's more trust, more clarity, and more human connection.

Leading Like a Symphony Conductor

Understand the plan, context, and key players in moving projects forward, like the symphony conductor who has skilled musicians, and perhaps a timeless score, and a wonderful hall but is the essential element in bringing it synergistically together. These conductors *bring their own style to the performance.*

Thus, they don't merely "execute," they deliver to the environment, each one different (and we haven't even included the audience, the customers, as yet). Their style seems to be contagious when successful, imbued in every musician and in every listener.

Projects are live performances, but there's no rehearsal. Improvisation is part of the craft, more like a jazz performance than a symphonic one. You need to understand the individual strengths and weaknesses of your team so that you can integrate them into a great harmony.

Empathy: The Underrated Superpower

Empathy here is the key. In Figure 2.2, you'll see the three dimensions of empathy. Mastering these elements enables you to better understand and appreciate team thinking, experiences, and emotions. *You need to trade airtime for insight and start listening to people.*

You can then influence better through understanding better. You only make your life harder when trying to coerce people, and then the big stick is no longer effective if it's gone or someone else has a bigger stick!

The formula: Influence = (Trust + Credibility + Connection) × Consistency. We're dealing with a thermostat you can control to set the temperature, and not an "on/off" switch. Motivation is intrinsic, and you can't motivate others, but you can create an environment that encourages their motivation applying empathy.

Experiential empathy means that I have shared your experience. Emotional empathy represents feeling what you are actually feeling. And intellectual empathy is the understanding of why you feel the way you do and the need to do something about it.

If you have:

1. Emotional empathy and experiential empathy, but not intellectual empathy, you don't see the need to act or reasons to do so.

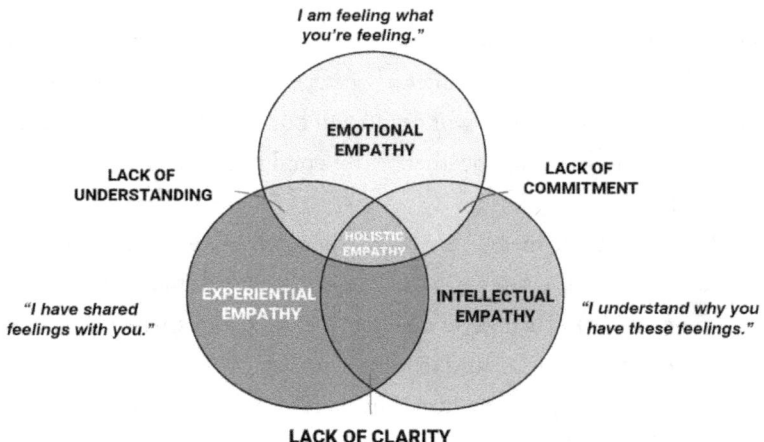

Figure 2.2 The empathy dimensions

2. Emotional empathy and intellectual empathy, but not experiential empathy, you don't truly understand from the other person's perspective.

3. Experiential empathy and intellectual empathy, but not emotional empathy, you aren't sufficiently engaged.

Thus, there is a need to truly engage with others to be able to lead and support them through the processes, purpose, and politics of any project. This is an enabler of the "influence formula" noted above.

What does "cultural thermostat" really mean and require? People in organizations mainly believe and act upon what they see. If they see a manager pausing to pick up trash on the floor, they will probably do so, themselves. If they see managers stopping their work and leaving at five on the dot, so will they.

Vignette: Two Examples From an Insurance Client

Two divisions across the hall from each other showed drastically different feedback on their assessment of the environment and management. One was a five on a five (high) to one scale. The other was a one. When I was asked to find out what was going on, arriving in the late afternoon, I wasn't even able to begin talking to anyone, but I noticed that the higher-ranking division followed their boss out at about 4:45 p.m., while the other followed theirs out at 5. Thus, the latter found it took far longer to get their cars out of the garage or to get to already-crowded trains and buses.

That was easily fixed with their mutual superior setting 5 p.m. as the departure time, come hell or high water.

In the second instance, the CEO was concerned about some complaints that newly insured people were billed too early. I found that the vice president of sales, after I confronted a few salespeople, was advocating that at the end of months, in order to ensure meeting quota, if new customers were unavailable to sign the new policies that their signatures be forged so that commissions were immediately payable.

The salespeople fearfully followed the executive's dictate. When I told the CEO, he went ballistic. The state insurance commissioner could have fined them or shut them down, and he fired the vice president in a senior management meeting to show what behavior he expected others to follow.

There is a "threshold effect" wherein people will endure long-term pain to avoid what is deemed higher immediate pain. (This is one reason people continue in horrible marriages, avoiding the divorce pain and "stain" and enduring the unhappiness.) In organizations, and with projects, people will often avoid confronting a superior or refusing to do something they know is illegal or unethical.

There is also the normative behavior, which urges people to go along with peers, no matter the issues. This is why brave people will run if all around them are running (or weak people will stay and fight if those around them stay and fight). It's why otherwise decent people caught up in riots wind up stealing merchandise themselves, because everyone around them is, and they want to be seen as supporting their peers.

How strong is watching exemplars or peers? People will become quite cynical when they hear one thing from an exemplar ("Customers are our most important asset") but see a contrary behavior (the executive refuses to take calls from customers and curses them out if they return things). So, we must model and reinforce, coach and reinforce, and set that thermostat to the desired temperature (behavior) in the room, and in the organization.

If culture is that set of beliefs that governs behaviors, we have to demonstrate the behaviors based on those beliefs. Let's see how that's done.

CHAPTER 3

Unlocking Team Magic

The Iceberg: What You Can't See Controls You

Before we can talk about team performance, we need to understand what's happening *beneath* it. That's where the iceberg we've discussed comes in. If you want to get people to behave differently, you need to shape the bottom of their iceberg.

You can't tell them to do this, because the best you'll get is superficial compliance. You need to engage their thinking to get them to reevaluate their beliefs and shift them willingly. Coaching is the bridge, discussed at the end of this chapter. For now, let's admit that fear is the great saboteur of success.

What's under the iceberg is what fuels fear. Decisions are often made based on emotion, not solely logic is often applied after the fact to justify the emotional decision. Here's an example of the "journey" required for change and the relevant decisions to achieve it. Figure 3.1 shows "the ambiguous zone":

You'll find that people are generally comfortable in their current state, but they will willingly consider an even better future state (people are not genetically opposed to change). But it's *the journey* that scares them and creates resistance. This is the psychology that excellent leaders must influence to help people commit to the journey, in effect proclaiming, "Don't worry, I know the way."

Project Pulse

Behaviors are manifestations of beliefs. To change the behaviors, change the beliefs.

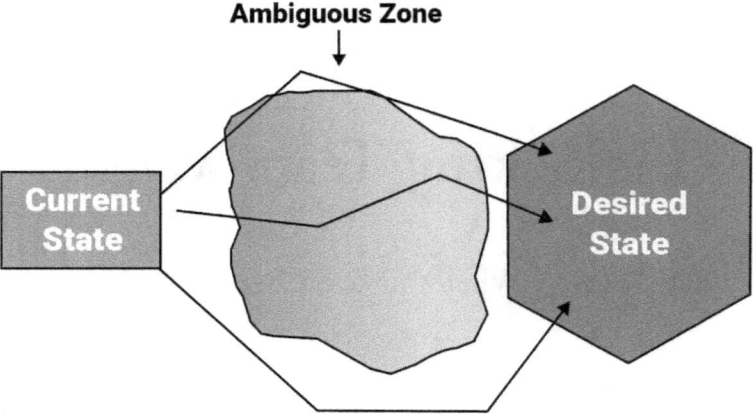

Figure 3.1 The ambiguous zone

Here's an exercise for you:

Step 1—Think of a recent decision you made quickly.
It could be small (buying a gadget, canceling plans) or big (turning down a job, ending a relationship). Something that felt like a "gut call."

Step 2—Write down your original reason.
What did you tell yourself (or others) about why you made that choice?

Step 3—Now pause, and ask yourself this:
What was I feeling in that moment? What emotion might have been driving me before the explanation kicked in?
Were you avoiding something? Seeking relief? Protecting your sense of competence? Chasing excitement?

Step 4—Connect the dots.
Often, the "reason" we give is just a logical wrapper around an emotional core. The brain makes the decision emotionally, and then the story follows.

How Fear Sabotages Success

The amygdala is always on the lookout for danger, like a smoke detector. When it detects something, it kicks in automatic responses, fight/flight/freeze. The body gets ready to survive the coming moments, heart rate increases, adrenaline shoots in, blood flow decreases to the brain and increases to the muscles. Cognitive function decreases, critical thinking slips away, and creativity disappears.

Then put this into the real world. Right when you need to perform at your best or need the best from someone, we default to applying pressure, inadvertently triggering a threat response that decreases performance right when we need people's best! Instead, we need to learn how to build an environment that reduces threat and increases reward; *that's when the best of your team is unlocked.*

Amy Edmondson's research on psychological safety makes one thing clear: The best teams don't just execute well, they communicate openly. In *The Fearless Organization*, she shows that high-performing teams are defined not by flawless planning or technical mastery, but by their ability to speak candidly, admit mistakes, and challenge one another's thinking without fear of embarrassment or blame. In environments where people feel safe to contribute honestly, cognitive resources stay online, and creativity, problem-solving, and learning flourish.

This directly counters the threat-response pattern: When people feel psychologically safe, they move out of defensiveness and into engagement. Leaders who want to unlock their team's potential must shift their focus from control to the surrounding conditions: from directing behavior to designing environments that reduce threat and increase reward.

This isn't just a theory. You've likely felt it too. When a team stops sharing ideas, it is not because they're lazy, but because the environment punishes risk-taking. Fear rarely announces itself clearly. More often, it hides behind logic, busyness, or the subtle urge to delay. Kursten reports: When I began this book, I didn't feel afraid in any obvious way. I felt busy. I told myself I needed more time to think, more research to do, more clarity before committing anything to the page.

Underneath all that, if I'm honest, was fear. Not panic but a quieter, more familiar kind of emotion. The kind that whispers: *What if this isn't good enough? What if no one wants to publish it?*

That's the trick with fear. It doesn't always pull the alarm. Sometimes, it quietly steers. It narrows our vision, dulls our creativity, and pushes us into the safety of preparation over action. I was working hard, but I wasn't writing. I was moving, but not making progress.

I caught myself in that loop several times. And I recognized it for what it was: a pattern driven by emotional autopilot. The system in me, designed to keep me safe, safe from rejection, from exposure, from getting it wrong, was doing its job a little too well!

That's when I made a choice. Not a grand, heroic decision. Just a small, intentional one: to keep going. To write even when it felt uncertain. Not because the fear disappeared, but because I was no longer willing to let it dictate the terms.

I share this not because writing a book is unique, but because the pattern is universal. When we move through fear with intention, when we notice the moment we're about to retreat, and choose instead to lean forward, we create the possibility of surprising ourselves. *Not with brilliance, but with the simple, quiet evidence that we're capable of more than we thought.*

Influence Brains, not Tasks

Once you understand the emotional filters in play, you can shape the stimuli that people respond to.

The longest second (so much happens in less than a second, and few people can see the steps): Stimulus is occurring which…

- Is filtered through our lens to create a story in our mind. We apply our experiences, expectations, and emotions to begin "sculpting" what is stimulating us (and perhaps determining fight, flight, or freeze).
- Creates emotional reactions (in the pit of the stomach or front of the mind).
- Initiates decisions made and rationalized.
- Ranges of actions as a result of the above.

Thus, your opportunity to influence others (and improve your own life) is to manage stimuli and shape stories to keep the threat low and the opportunity high so that better decisions can be made.

There are opportunities every day to show people your intentions, capitalize on them to keep the fear down, and increase the trust in the environment. This is what I call "show, don't tell."

In other words, show people WIIFM—What's In It For Me? This is one of the most powerful lenses through which people interpret communication. Whether consciously or unconsciously, every person evaluates information based on how it affects them, their goals, their comfort, and their sense of identity or status. When leaders ignore this, they risk triggering resistance or disengagement. But when you frame your message with WIIFM in mind by clearly linking your request, change, or idea to something the other person values, you reduce threat, increase buy-in, and create a bridge between your intent and their motivation. It's not manipulation; it's meeting people where they are.

Project Pulse

People change based on perceived personal best interests being met, not necessarily your best interests.

Example: Coaching conversation helping someone appreciate WIIFM

Coach: "I noticed you seemed hesitant when the leadership opportunity came up. Can I ask, What are you thinking about that?"

Jordan: "Honestly, I've got too much on my plate. And I'm not sure stepping into that role is worth it."

Coach: "Totally fair. Can we explore that a bit? What would make something like this *worth it* for you?"

Jordan: [pauses] "I guess if it helped me grow... if it moved me closer to doing more strategic work, not just tactical execution."

Coach: "That's helpful to hear. In your view, what kinds of experiences tend to lead to more strategic roles?"

Jordan: "Probably leading bigger initiatives, influencing direction, being seen by decision-makers."

Coach: "And how close—or far—does this opportunity feel from that kind of experience?"

Jordan: [thinking] "...Closer than I thought, actually. I hadn't made that connection."

Coach: "What would need to be true for you to say yes to this with clarity and confidence?"

Example: Showing a team member the WIIFM

In my early 30s, I left corporate life to start a boutique consultancy. The business grew quickly, and within a year, I had a team of 10. From the outside, it looked like success. But inside, I was scrambling to keep up. I had no playbook for how to truly lead people, especially when things got hard. I found myself in a crash course on coaching, influence, and learning to meet people where they are.

One experience stands out.

A high-performing team member began to decline, subtly at first. A missed detail here, a withdrawn comment there. Eventually, I realized that the person was facing serious mental health challenges. I wanted to help, so I did what many well-meaning leaders do: I pushed. I encouraged them to get help, go to therapy, and take action. And they did ... once. But they came back with excuses for why it wasn't for them. *I had treated it like a problem to be solved. But there was no ownership, only compliance.* And so, nothing really changed.

That's when I realized I was trying to shortcut the process. I was prescribing a solution instead of helping them discover their own. So I stepped back and shifted into coaching mode. I began asking questions not about symptoms or solutions, but about what they wanted in their life, what kind of future they imagined, and what "better" might look like on their terms. In doing that, I helped them connect to their own *why*, the personal WIIFM.

From there, we worked together to chart next steps. They weren't the steps I would have chosen. The route wasn't linear or efficient. But they owned them. And I knew that **forward progress on a winding path is better than no progress or worse, retreating into old patterns.**

Eventually, they made the decision to engage health care providers again. This time it was not because I said to do so, but because they saw it as the best way to move toward the life that was actually desired. The results were astonishing. Their energy returned and clarity grew. Performance soared to levels I hadn't seen before and not out of obligation, but from purpose.

That moment changed how I lead. It taught me that ***real transformation doesn't come from pressure; it comes from insight.*** When people feel safe enough to reflect, and supported enough to act, they can find a way forward that's truly their own. And that's the path they gladly travel.

From Boss to Coach: The Art of Building Giants

If you want to build giants, you need to get out of the way of their growth, and that means shifting from boss to coach.

Coaching is your "boots on the ground" approach to shift people's thinking, help them grow, and increase their performance. Coaching isn't "telling" someone what to do. It's communicating in an influential way to get people to reevaluate their beliefs and attitudes and chart a different course. (Remember the old admonition to teach people how to catch fish, don't catch the fish for them, or they'll always look to you to do their job? If you do other people's jobs, it becomes "failure work," and soon you'll be exhausted doing *everyone's* jobs.)

Give someone something they already understand and use that as the bridge to help them understand a new concept.

Example: Driving to work

Most of us have had the experience of driving to work and arriving without remembering much of the drive. We were alert enough to stay in our lane and stop at red lights but weren't fully conscious of every turn. We were running on habit, muscle memory, and familiar patterns.

Work is often the same. People show up, go through the motions, respond to challenges, and perform without always being aware of the underlying choices they're making. They're reacting from learned behaviors, past experiences, and emotional patterns that rarely get examined. (This is called "unconscious competency," just as we don't have to concentrate when tying shoelaces or putting on a watch.)

A coaching conversation is like asking someone to pull over and look at the map. (Thus, we drive them back so "conscious competency": To tie your shoe, make a knot, then a loop….")

"Is this the best route? Do you even want to go where you're heading? What if there's another way you haven't seen or considered yet?"

Coach: "Have you ever driven somewhere familiar, like your commute to work, and arrived without really remembering the drive?"
Coachee: "Yeah, all the time."
Coach: "What do you think makes that happen?"
Coachee: "I guess it's just routine, I'm not really thinking."

Coach: "Do you think any part of your workday feels like that right now?"

Coachee: [pauses] "Maybe. I feel like I'm going through the motions in meetings."

Coach: "What might be one area where you've been operating on autopilot… that, if you were more intentional, could shift your results or how you feel?"

Here's how the full sequence looks:

Unconscious competency

Conscious competency

Conscious incompetency

Unconscious incompetency

At the bottom, we don't know that a shoe needs to be tied or a job needs to be done. At the second, we know what needs to be done, but can't do it. At the third, we learn to do it by steps and repetition. And at the top, we do it without thinking about it, as that drive, or as that job.

Project Pulse

We can only learn in conscious competency, so we have to drive people back to that stage in order to effectively coach them and for them to effectively learn.

Example: A Coaching Giant in the Mainstream: Phil Jackson

If there's a mainstream example of coaching leadership that mirrors this shift from control to insight, it's Phil Jackson. Known as the "Zen Master" of the NBA (National Basketball Association in the United States), Jackson didn't just win games; he transformed how teams functioned. With 11 championship titles as head coach of the Chicago Bulls and Los Angeles Lakers, Jackson coached some of the most iconic (and ego-bloated) players in history, including Michael Jordan, Scottie Pippen, Kobe Bryant, and Shaquille O'Neal. But his brilliance wasn't in strategy alone; it was in psychology.

Jackson prioritized mindset over mechanics. He introduced his teams to mindfulness, used storytelling and Native American teachings to communicate values, and focused relentlessly on helping players understand themselves and each other. He rarely barked orders. Instead, he asked questions that invited reflection, drew on metaphors to reframe challenges, and created space for ownership to emerge. Even with towering talent on the floor, he knew performance wasn't unlocked through pressure, but through trust, internal alignment, and shared meaning.

His approach is a real-world proof point: The most successful teams are not the ones with the most control from the top; they are the ones where leaders coach insight at the bottom. Jackson didn't force greatness out of his players; he created the conditions for it to emerge.

His coaching model included:

- listen to gather info
- ask questions to generate insight
- help others translate to actionable next steps
- facilitate self-evaluation of action and results
- demonstrate this is circular, not linear

Vignette: Contrasting Coaching Styles

Dan calls Sasha into his office. He doesn't sit down. Doesn't ask a question. Just starts in:

> "That presentation was unacceptable. You weren't prepared. We've talked about raising the bar, and this missed it. You need to tighten things up fast, our clients expect excellence."
>
> Sasha's jaw tightens. Her face flushes. She nods, mutters "Got it," and leaves.
>
> Inside, she feels shame. Frustration. Pressure. She goes back to her desk and starts reworking the deck, but she's focused on **avoiding another blow-up**, not understanding the real gaps. She becomes more tentative, second-guesses herself, and avoids asking for help.
>
> Dan achieved compliance. Not growth.

Same situation. Different leader. Morgan also brings Sasha into her office—but invites her to sit down.

"Can I ask, "how did you feel that meeting went?"

Sasha hesitates, then admits she felt rushed and unsure.

Morgan listens. Then asks:

"What do you think the client was hoping to see that we didn't quite deliver?"

They unpack the assumptions Sasha made. Morgan doesn't offer answers; she keeps asking questions. Sasha starts to see the gaps herself.

Then Morgan asks:

"What's one way you might frame the proposal differently next time?"

They co-create a plan. At the end, Morgan says:

"Would you be open to reflecting on how that plan landed after the next meeting? I'd love to support your learning curve."

Sasha leaves energized. Curious. She isn't just fixing a slide, she's improving how she thinks.

Dan focused on performance through control. Morgan focused on performance through a shift in thinking. And that's what real coaching leadership is about.

You don't unlock teams through control. You do it by changing the stories they tell themselves, one insight at a time.

Let's examine how ownership of this process can be imbued in teams.

CHAPTER 4

Ownership:
The Hidden Multiplier

Teams that lack ownership tend to "stall." You can issue instructions, enforce deadlines, and track compliance, *but you'll spend enormous energy maintaining minimal momentum.* True commitment doesn't come from checklists. It comes when people choose to own the outcome. That's when they bring their creativity, critical thinking, and full humanity to the work.

Ownership can't be commanded, only cultivated. It's the invisible multiplier that transforms task-driven teams into problem-solving engines. When leaders create the conditions for ownership to grow, innovation takes root, collaboration deepens, and performance becomes self-sustaining. This chapter shows you how to spark that shift, from managing tasks to unlocking team magic.

Story: My personal introduction into a hidden world

My first coach asked me a question I'll never forget: "What's the difference between ownership and accountability?" I paused, fumbled around for a half-answer about responsibility and follow-through, but the truth was I didn't really know. I thought they were the same thing. At the time, I naively believed that if you told someone what to do, and they nodded along, they'd just go and do it. Easy, right? But over time, I started noticing a pattern: People would smile, agree, and then...nothing would happen. At first, I blamed them. But slowly, the penny dropped. There was a choice being made not just by them, but by me, too. And that choice was ownership.

What I came to learn was that accountability is external, something we assign. But ownership? That's internal and it's personal. It's treating the outcome like your name is stamped on it. That coach helped me see that

I couldn't force ownership by assigning tasks or setting deadlines. What I could do was create the conditions for it: check for real understanding, ask questions that evoke commitment, and slow down enough to sense whether someone has truly bought in. I started learning to spot the difference between nodding heads and engaged hearts.

That shift wasn't just tactical; it was foundational. It changed how I saw people and my role as a leader. *I had to let go of the belief that people were programmable*, like robots you could instruct into action. Instead, I began to see them as equals with their own unique thinking, values, and ways of making sense of the world. My job wasn't to micromanage or delegate tasks, but to help them discover the opportunity for themselves, build their capacity for critical thinking, and create the space for learning and experimentation. That belief changed everything: how I communicated, how I listened, and how I measured success.

Project Pulse

Leadership became less about control and more about cultivation.

Why Teams Without Ownership Stall

Teams stall not because people are lazy or incapable, but because they don't see a reason to care. Ownership requires psychological investment: the belief that this matters and that I have a meaningful part to play in it. Too often, however, people don't make that investment. Why? Because of fear, disconnection, or simply not seeing the point. Ownership is a choice, and people only make it when the risk feels worth the reward, emotionally, psychologically, and personally.

Sometimes it's fear of failure or judgment, "If I really care and it goes badly, that's on me." Sometimes it's the belief that decisions are made far above their pay grade, so why bother trying? Sometimes it's because no one has ever helped them connect their work to a purpose they believe in. Other times, it's a lack of skill, particularly critical thinking skills. Without that connection, to meaning, agency, or competence, people default to self-protection and minimal compliance. They wait to be told, hedge their bets, and keep their heads down.

The result? Momentum slows. Initiative dies. Projects stall. Not because people don't have the capacity, but because the system has never invited their full participation and/or they aren't brave enough to take the risk.

The costs of not building ownership:

- Reduced return on investment made in projects
- Failing to achieve strategic goals and direction is chaotic, like magnets each with their own north pole; organizational sustainability is at risk
- Decisions bottlenecked by senior resources slowing down achievement of value
- Senior resources focused on low-level tasks and decisions rather than leading toward the big picture

One cannot demand ownership, only compliance. Compliance versus ownership:

- Compliance: I do what I'm told and no more.
- Accountability: I'm held responsible if it doesn't happen.
- Ownership: I care about making it happen because I believe in it.

You can command timesheets in on time, being on time for work, meeting deadlines, and people can prove that minimum compliance.

Ownership occurs when people unlock their creativity, innovation, and problem-solving to achieve valuable outcomes, and no one can force this. It's where real value creation lies.

Commitment is the bridge between compliance and ownership and is the point where the choice is made, shifting from low-value task focus to unlocking critical thinking, creativity, and innovation to achieve outcomes that exponentially grow value.

Leading to build ownership is like gardening: planting seeds that give people the opportunity and choice. Water and fertilizing are coaching, support, and feedback, and sunlight is a shared purpose that draws people forward, bearing fruit, the result of ownership.

The Foundations of Ownership: Self-Determination Theory

If ownership is a choice, what needs to be true for someone to make that choice? According to psychologists Edward Deci and Richard Ryan,[1] intrinsic motivation, the kind that leads to deep engagement, persistence, and care, is built on three essential psychological needs: autonomy, competence, and relatedness. These aren't management buzzwords. They're basic human drivers. Picture a three-legged stool: remove one, and motivation becomes unstable. Without all three, ownership collapses.

Autonomy is the feeling that your choices are your own. It's not just about freedom; it's about agency. When people feel like they're merely executing someone else's plan, motivation shrinks. But when they believe they have a voice, discretion, and room to experiment, they engage differently. Autonomy isn't the absence of structure, but rather it's the presence of trust.

Competence is the belief that you're capable and effective, in that you have the skills to succeed or the support to grow. When people feel constantly out of their depth or under-resourced, they pull back to protect themselves. But when they feel appropriately challenged and see progress, they lean in. Competence is about building momentum through mastery.

Relatedness is the sense of connection to others, to the mission, or to something meaningful beyond the task. When people feel isolated, anonymous, or disconnected from purpose, they disengage. But when they feel like part of something that matters, they bring more of themselves. Relatedness is the emotional glue that turns task completion into commitment. You can see in Figure 4.1 what happens if you don't have all three "lets":

Competence and relatedness without autonomy limit actions. Competence and autonomy without relatedness produce irrelevance. And autonomy and relatedness without competence create "spinning wheels" and no movement.

As a leader, your job is to select and develop people with these three building blocks in mind. When hiring or forming teams, you're not just looking for skills; you're looking for alignment: Does this person want

---

[1] *Self-Determination Theory*, Plenum Publishing, 2000.

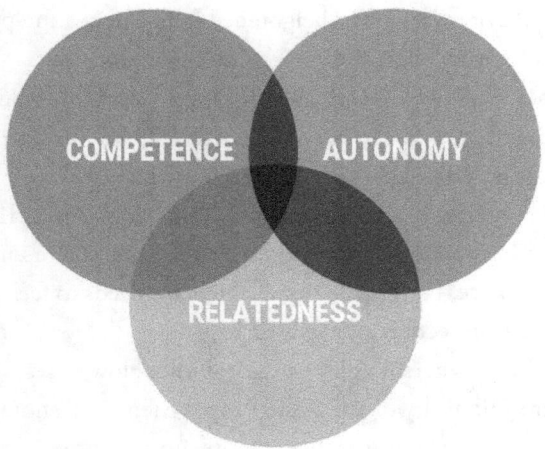

Figure 4.1 The ownership support structures

autonomy? Are they open to growth? Can they connect to purpose or team mission? These qualities aren't fixed; they can be nurtured. But the raw material has to be there.

Once someone is on the team, your role is to cultivate these elements over time. That means giving people room to shape their work (autonomy), supporting them to develop skill and confidence (competence), and connecting their effort to meaning and relationships (relatedness). These are the conditions where ownership can take root and thrive.

Sometimes, it becomes clear that a person isn't aligned with this kind of environment because they resist autonomy, reject feedback, or stay detached from purpose despite real effort to help them engage. In those cases, you're not doing anyone a favor by dragging them along. Ownership isn't something you can force on someone; it must be chosen. Your responsibility as a leader is to create a team environment where ownership is possible, and to protect that environment by ensuring the people in it are willing and able to step into it.

A "Flow State" may be the ultimate gateway to peak performance.

There's a rare and powerful state many of us have experienced—often without knowing how we got there. It's that moment when time seems to vanish, distractions fade, and you become fully absorbed in what you're doing. That's flow, which is a term coined by psychologist Mihaly

Csikszentmihalyi[2] to describe a heightened state of focus and performance where effort feels effortless, and productivity is at its peak.

But here's what most people miss: Flow is impossible when the brain is in a state of threat. When people are stressed, afraid of being blamed, or constantly on edge, the nervous system shifts into protection mode. Executive functioning narrows, creativity shuts down, and critical thinking collapses into basic task execution. In this state, there's no room for flow, only vigilance. For flow to occur, the brain needs to feel safe enough to let go of self-protection and fully engage.

That's where ownership plays a critical role. Flow arises when people are doing meaningful work that challenges them just enough, not too easy, not too overwhelming. Even more importantly, it arises when they feel psychologically safe, personally invested, and cognitively free. Ownership fosters that investment. When someone sees the work as theirs, when they feel trusted and supported to solve real problems in their own way, their focus sharpens. Their energy aligns. They're able to find that elusive zone where their skills and the challenge are in perfect balance.

Flow can't be forced, but it can be cultivated. Leaders who create the conditions for ownership are also creating the conditions for flow. Not by adding pressure, but by removing fear. Not by micromanaging, but by setting clear outcomes and letting people find their own way there. When they do, what follows isn't just productivity, it's a breakthrough. It's that unmistakable feeling of deep work, deep purpose, and deep satisfaction, where people don't just get more done, they become more of who they are capable of being.

Story: *Leaving It All on the Ice*

I used to play competitive sports, and looking back, some of my clearest experiences of flow came on the ice. There were games when everything clicked, not because I was dominating the scoreboard, but because I was completely immersed. The noise of the crowd faded, my mind stopped racing, and I was fully present, reading the play, anticipating

---

[2] *Flow*, Harper & Row, 1990.

movements, reacting without overthinking. It didn't mean I won every game like that, but whenever I found that state, I knew I had left everything I had out there.

Those moments were deeply satisfying, not because of the outcome, but because of the experience of being "all in." The intensity of focus and the feeling of control and trust in my instincts made it feel as if time stood still or even vanished completely. More than once, I stepped off the ice and was shocked to find the sun had set. I'd walk out of the rink into darkness, having completely lost track of time. It wasn't just physical exertion; it was full mental and emotional engagement.

That's what flow feels like. And once you've touched it, you start to chase it. not for the sake of productivity, but for the integrity of the experience itself. It's a reminder of what's possible when you care deeply, feel challenged, and have the freedom to bring your full self to the moment.

Behavior leaves clues

When there is a lack of ownership:

- People escalate decisions they could have made themselves
- Meetings have low value, updates instead of problem-solving
- Reactive rather than proactive decisions are predominant
- Little creativity occurs, and little energy is invested in it
- The same roadblocks keep appearing, as if no one has learned anything about that road
- Defensiveness and blame take precedence over cause and improvements
- "That's not my job" echoes through the halls

But when you create healthy ownership:

- Team members anticipate and take action
- Barriers are navigated rather than seen as impenetrable, for example, cross-functional conflict
- Feedback and coaching flow are normal activities
- People move forward without waiting for approval on things that provide value (It's easier to get forgiveness than permission)

- Dialogue changes to outcome-focused rather than task-focused
- Conflict arises from passion around the investment in the work, which is a positive dynamic

---

Project Pulse

"The most deeply motivated people – not to mention those who are most productive and satisfied – hitch their desires to a cause larger than themselves." —Dan Pink

---

Exposing the "Fake Superstars"

"Fake superstars" are often celebrated for their high output. They work fast, produce visibly, and often take on a heroic glow in moments of crisis. But under the surface, *they operate on self-interest, not shared purpose.* Their contributions aren't multiplied by the team. They're extracted from it.

They want the credit, avoid accountability, and see colleagues as tools or obstacles. The short-term gain they offer is often outweighed by the long-term damage: psychological safety erodes, collaboration stalls, and team morale fractures. People around them retreat into self-preservation and are disengaged, misaligned, and unwilling to take risks. You're left with a few finished tasks and a trail of broken trust.

In my early 20s, I strutted into project management with the swagger of someone who thought he had it all figured out. My to-do lists were long, my inbox always buzzing, and I equated "busy" with "valuable." I believed productivity was about grinding harder, checking boxes, and expecting others to match my pace. When people didn't deliver after smiling and nodding in meetings, I saw it as a character flaw, not a leadership issue. Bonuses and recognition were my go-to tools for motivation, but they landed flat. I couldn't understand why no one seemed as fired up as I was. In my mind, I was the rockstar, hard-working, driven, and getting things done. However, under the spotlight, I was faking it. The applause I craved never came, and I started to hit walls I couldn't break through.

Then came the shift. I stumbled, more by desperation than design, into the world of social psychology and neuroscience. And what I saw in the mirror wasn't a superstar, but a guy unintentionally building an environment of pressure and compliance rather than trust and choice. I started learning how to create safety, how to listen without fixing, how to invite participation instead of commanding it. Slowly, I let go of the ego that needed to be the smartest or the busiest in the room. And something powerful happened: people started showing up, not for me, but with me. My leadership changed, not because I had better answers, but because I was finally asking better questions. And for the first time, I wasn't faking anything.

Fake Superstars Fool Us

Many fake superstars thrive under leaders who measure performance through task volume, not value creation. They look impressive when you're only tracking to-do lists. Instead, ask how well they elevate others, solve the right problems, or align with broader goals, and their shine fades. (You might call these "to accomplish lists.")

- High Output, low-value contribution
- Want all the glory for themselves but are not aligned with the best value to the organization
- Behaviors are self-serving and misaligned but often mistaken as highly productive and valuable
- They leave a trail of finished tasks and broken people
- Destruction of safety
- Resulting costs: turnover, disengagement, and self-preservation become normalized behaviors for those around the superstar

Behavioral traits:

- They value being right over being relational.
- They see people as problems instead of partners.
- Highly value getting work done as directly as possible without consideration for others.

- Can't see the big picture.
- They equate control with competence and resist shared ownership.
- They want others to work the way they do ("Clone me" syndrome). You may hear, "if only I could clone myself."

What real contributors look like

- Systemic opportunity, build systems, relationships, and people's abilities instead of task completion
- Raise others up, not just themselves
- Take accountability and invite feedback
- Speak up when the stakes are important even when it's uncomfortable
- Contribute without casting shadows
- Align the team on goals, outcomes, and metrics that advance the organization

Case Study: Microsoft's Coaching Culture

One of the most well-known examples of shifting from a culture of individual heroism to one of shared ownership and growth comes from Microsoft. Under CEO Satya Nadella's leadership, Microsoft made a deliberate move away from a "know-it-all" culture toward a "learn-it-all" mindset. This wasn't just a slogan because it was a full cultural reset. Managers were no longer rewarded for simply hitting metrics or demonstrating technical dominance. Instead, they were evaluated on how well they coached their teams, fostered collaboration, and modeled curiosity. The focus moved from being the smartest person in the room to creating rooms where everyone felt safe and equipped to contribute.

If you want to work in leadership at Microsoft today, especially as a manager or senior leader, you'd better show up with a coaching mindset. The expectation is clear: your job is to grow people, not to have all the right answers. If you're still operating from a command-and-control approach, if your value comes from telling rather than developing, you won't thrive there. This coaching culture was embedded into performance reviews, development programs, and everyday leadership conversations. Managers were trained to ask better questions, listen actively, and elevate the thinking of others. The result was a dramatic increase in trust, innovation, and engagement, and a redefinition of what strong, modern leadership really looks like.

Exercise: Who gets celebrated on your team? And for what?

- Take 5 minutes and reflect honestly:
  o Who have you publicly praised in the last month? Write down two to three names.
- What were you celebrating in each case?
  o For example, speed? Volume? Bravery? Collaboration? Creativity? Clean execution under pressure? Even a great idea that failed?
- Were their contributions aligned with team success, or individual visibility?
  o Did they *raise the bar* for others, or just hit their own targets?
- What message might that praise have sent to the rest of the team?
  o Should others "be like this person"? Is that the culture you want?
- Now ask yourself:
  o Are the people who elevate others, solve hard problems, and lead with integrity getting noticed too, or are they quietly keeping the team afloat while someone else gets the spotlight?
- This exercise isn't about blame; it's about bringing awareness to the behaviors you're reinforcing. Over time, what you reward becomes what your team repeats: The unwritten rules that everyone plays by, that is, *the culture*.

How to do it differently by aligning behaviors:

- Cocreate the north star, the values you'll live by, and behavioral examples of what it looks like to "show up."
- Use the value framework to explore actual examples of behavior in coaching conversations to generate insights on alignment.

- Don't reward output without context, both behavioral and environmental.
- Be willing to have the hard conversation when high performers also cause high collateral damage.
- Remove people who won't align with the value framework regardless of their task productivity.

Stay Out of the Drama Triangle

This thrives where ownership is absent. It's powered by blame and self-preservation, not ownership and collaboration. It's inversely correlated with ownership of outcomes, which isn't hard to understand.

Karpman's[3] psychological and social model includes:

- Victim
- Rescuer
- Persecutor

People caught in this dynamic shift among being victim, rescuer, and persecutor without improvement in themselves of the situation as outlined in Figure 4.2 below.

This reinforces self-serving beliefs by creating negative dynamics and interactions. People need to see outside the triangle if they are to achieve something bigger. To break the triangle:

People need to see outside the triangle if they are to achieve something bigger. Model and reward behaviors aligned with taking risks, speaking up, experimentation, learning, and taking accountability for one's self, especially by shifting conversations:

- Instead of who's to blame—What can we learn?
- Instead of how do I fix this for you—What are your options and what do you recommend?
- Instead of why is this happening to me—What's in your control and choices do you have?

---

[3] *The Karpman Drama Triangle,* CWTK Publications, 2020.

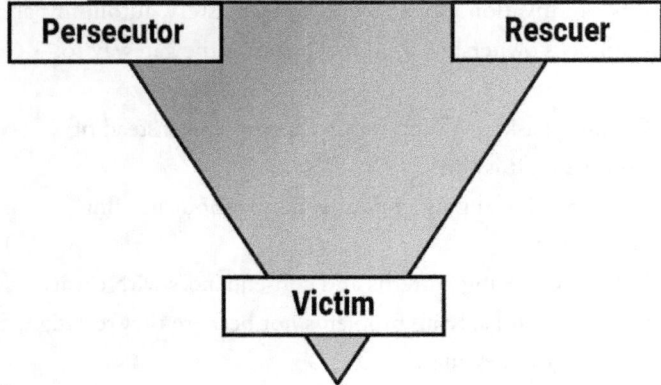

Figure 4.2 Karpman's triangle

How Critical Thinking Blooms From Ownership

Ownership is the ignition key to critical thinking. Without it, you're just sitting in the driver's seat, engine off, waiting for someone else to tell you where to go. When people feel true ownership over their work, their learning, and their outcomes, they begin to think more deeply, challenge assumptions, and make better decisions. They stop "outsourcing" responsibility and start activating the part of themselves that is willing to wrestle with uncertainty.

Extrinsic motivators like bonuses, deadlines, and fear of failure can drive action, but not insight. *They incentivize minimum compliance, not maximum contribution.* People do just enough to earn the reward or avoid the consequence. There's no room or reason for thinking critically, let alone creatively.

Project Pulse

The only true motivation is intrinsic, but you can build environments that foster it.

Carrots and sticks are outdated. They keep people in transactional mode, not transformational growth. When rewards are external, thinking stays external too. People wait to be told what's right instead of figuring it out themselves.

Intrinsic motivation, driven by purpose, mastery, autonomy, and connection, unlocks ownership. And ownership is the gateway to:

- Curiosity: asking "Why is this happening?" instead of "Whose fault is this?"
- Courage: challenging the status quo without needing permission
- Reflection: seeing patterns and consequences with clarity
- Commitment: solving problems not because they're assigned, but because they matter

If you want a team of problem-solvers, not passive executors, stop managing for compliance and start leading for ownership.

Ownership isn't a bonus feature, it's the engine. Without it, the smartest strategy won't stick, and the best people won't stay. The real work of leadership is creating the conditions where ownership becomes not just possible, but natural. Where people don't just do the job, they become the architects of something they believe in. *And that's your job.*

So ask yourself: Where am I modeling ownership? Where might I still be clinging to control? What would it look like to trust people enough to let them lead, even when it's messy?

That's going to require some critical thinking....

CHAPTER 5

Critical Thinking: Think Like a Master Strategist

The quality of your thinking determines the clarity of your path, the results you achieve, and the value you deliver. Don't follow your outdated road signs blindly; you need to constantly be redrawing them.

Better Decisions = Faster Success

Project momentum is driven not by effort alone, but by how quickly and effectively decisions get made. Decisions require quality and velocity. Work does not move at the pace of effort. *It moves at the pace of decisions.*

Most people confuse activity with progress. They assume that putting in more hours, adding more meetings, or working harder will accelerate outcomes. But the real bottleneck is almost always decision making. Until a decision is made, no meaningful forward motion can happen. Energy gets trapped in ambiguity, waiting for clarity.

The speed and quality of decision making set the limit for how fast a project can progress. When decisions are clear, timely, and aligned, momentum builds. When decisions are delayed, avoided, or muddled, everything slows down regardless of how many people are working long hours.

That is why velocity depends not on effort, but on clarity. And clarity comes from having the right people trusted to make the right calls, with the right information, at the right time. Leaders who focus on efficiency often try to optimize labor. But the real leverage is not the number of hands on deck. It is the sharpness and timeliness of the decisions those hands are waiting for.

If you want to move faster, do not ask who needs to work harder. Ask what decisions are stuck, who is avoiding them, and what needs to be known to move forward with confidence.

Project Pulse

When teams use words like clarity, alignment, or just to confirm, it can sound reasonable, even responsible. But listen closely. These words often signal hesitation. They are placeholders for the fear of getting it wrong.

When clarity becomes the team's dominant need, it usually means people are waiting. They are holding back. They want someone else to make the decision, to eliminate the risk, and to guarantee the outcome before taking action.

Beneath that surface is a mindset that values precision over progress and safety over momentum. It feels careful, maybe even professional. But in practice, it slows everything down.

If your team is always asking for clarity, it might be a sign that no one is leading. Excellent outcomes begin with a strong decision-making process, as seen in Figure 5.1.

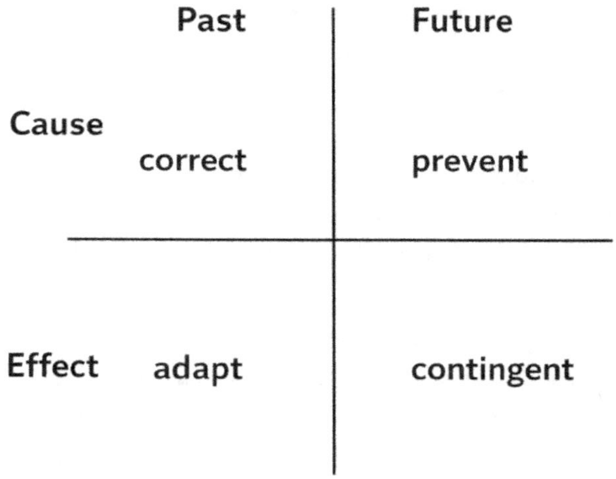

Figure 5.1 Decision categories

Good thinkers focus on the decision process over the outcome alone. In Figure 5.1, the upper left quadrant denotes that to remove an existing problem, you must know and correct the cause. If the roof is leaking, you repair the hole. That's corrective, restoring the former conditions. In the bottom right, you might know the cause or you don't care to fix it, so you put a bucket under the leak, you adapt (or you put oil into the car's engine once a month instead of repairing the engine to stop the oil leak).

In the upper right, you prevent future problems by preventing the cause: If fire can be caused by smoking, you erect nonsmoking signs; if by combustibles, you separate the combustibles. But if the preventive isn't effective and the problem occurs anyway, you use contingent actions (bottom right) to deal with the symptoms: insurance, sprinklers, and escape routes. (Interestingly, if you ask most people what to do in the event of a potential fire, they almost always give priority to contingent and not preventive actions, which is a fundamental decision flaw.)

We have to let go of being "perfect" as a legitimate goal. The hunt for perfection slows progress and undermines excellence. "Good" gets you moving. "Great" comes through iteration. "Excellence" is iteration and continual improvement. And "perfection" is a chimera.

The Difference Between a Miss and a Mistake. In Figure 5.2, you'll see the relationship of good and bad decisions based on being right or being lucky.

We often treat outcomes as the final verdict on a decision, but that is a dangerous oversimplification. *Just because something worked does not mean it was smart.* And just because something failed does not mean it was a mistake. The real question is whether the decision was sound at the time it was made.

I use this simple quadrant to help teams separate luck from judgment. On one axis, you have good versus bad decisions. This reflects the quality of thinking, intent, and process. On the other axis, you have right versus wrong outcomes. These are the results that unfold afterward. A good decision with the right outcome is a strategic win. A good decision with a wrong outcome is still an intelligent risk. You thought it through, accepted the possibility of failure, and made the call. That is what decision making under uncertainty looks like.

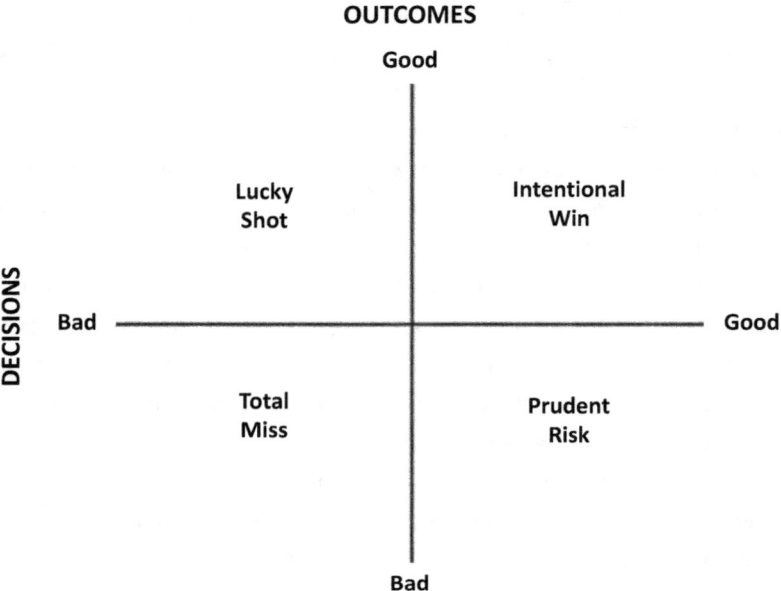

Figure 5.2 Relationships of quality of decision and quality of outcome

Good + right = Intentional win
Good + wrong = intelligent risk
Bad + right = lucky shot
Bad + wrong = total miss

A bad decision with the right outcome is a lucky shot. It worked, but it teaches nothing and cannot be repeated with confidence. And a bad decision with a wrong outcome is a total miss. Poor reasoning, weak process, and failure at every level.

You want to live in the upper half of that chart. Focus on making good decisions, knowing that some will still turn out wrong because you cannot control results. What you can control is the quality of your thinking. Every good decision begins with one key question. Can I live with this if it does not work? If the answer is yes, you are on solid ground. If the answer is no, you are gambling.

Risk Isn't Hermetically Sealed—It's Alive

Most teams treat risk as a compliance task. But real risk is dynamic and embodied. It lives or dies based on *how people behave*.

Case Study: What the Autobahn Teaches us About Real-Time Risk

In most organizations, risk is treated like a box-checking exercise. It gets identified early, recorded neatly, and then forgotten. But risk doesn't live in spreadsheets. It lives in motion. It shifts constantly, shaped by awareness, context, and human behavior.

Few places demonstrate this better than Germany's Autobahn.

At first glance, the system seems reckless. Many sections have no posted speed limit. You'd expect that to make it more dangerous than the heavily regulated highways of North America.

But the reality is quite different.

Germany's motorway fatality rate, including on unrestricted Autobahn sections, is around 1.36 deaths per billion vehicle kilometers.[1] In the United States, it's closer to 4.13 deaths per billion vehicle kilometers.[2] That's three times higher, even with strict speed enforcement.

The Autobahn isn't safer because it lacks rules. It's safer because it's a smarter, more adaptive system. Germany treats risk as something alive and responsive. They adjust in real time. Here's what that looks like:

- Driver training: Becoming a licensed driver in Germany involves extensive and expensive training. Drivers are taught high-speed handling, situational awareness, and lane discipline.
- Road design: The Autobahn is built for speed. It features long curves, wide lanes, limited intersections, and clear signage.

---

[1] BASt International Traffic and Accident Data 2025.
[2] BASt International Traffic and Accident Data 2025.

- Selective enforcement: Speed may not be limited, but behavior is. Tailgating, unsafe passing, and blocking lanes are strictly penalized. Trucks have lane and speed restrictions.
- Cultural norms: German drivers cooperate. They pass and return to the right lane. They stay focused. They respect the flow of traffic.
- Real-time adjustments: Most importantly, the system reacts. When conditions change due to weather, construction, or crashes, dynamic speed limits are activated immediately. Risk is acknowledged and recalibrated, not ignored.

I experienced this for myself on a drive from Munich to Innsbruck. What struck me wasn't just the quality of the road, but the rhythm of the traffic. It moved like a symphony. Three lanes of cars traveling at different speeds yet perfectly synchronized. Even through the mountain passes, where conditions varied, no one acted erratically. Drivers were respectful, aware, and cooperative. It felt fast, but not dangerous. It felt alive.

Where I grew up, the approach was very different. If there was a crash on a highway, the speed limit in that area was usually lowered permanently. There was no analysis of what actually caused the accident. No consideration of driver skill, weather conditions, vehicle quality, or tire choice. Just a blanket assumption that speed was to blame. So we slowed everything down indefinitely.

That kind of thinking is common in organizations too.

Project Pulse

Do you adjust dynamically or create unbreakable rules based on nonexistent conditions?

When a project fails to deliver on time, the response is often to add more approvals. When a budget is exceeded, leaders tighten every line item. When someone makes a mistake, a new policy is introduced. Complexity is met with more constraints. Risk management becomes a matter of adding friction instead of increasing capability.

But that's not how real safety or progress works.

Like the Autobahn, truly effective systems don't rely on rigid limitations. They build in situational awareness. They equip people to respond, not just comply. They elevate skill, strengthen feedback loops, and adapt to changing conditions.

Instead of asking "What's the limit here?", project leaders should ask:

"What's the actual risk, and how can we raise awareness rather than just lower speed?"

When we start treating risk as a living force that demands active attention, we move faster, safer, and with far less waste.

Let's examine what I call "1st, 2nd, and 3rd order thinking."

One of the biggest traps in decision making is stopping at the first layer. Most people think only in terms of immediate consequences. They do what seems obvious, sensible, and safe. The problem is, the obvious choice is often a shallow one. First-order thinking is reactive. Strategic thinking begins at the third.

Let's use another driving metaphor.

First-order thinking is seeing that a car in front of you is slowing down, so you hit the brakes. Immediate, necessary, and basic.

Second-order thinking is realizing that if traffic is building up, there's probably a slowdown ahead, so you start scanning for exits or alternate routes.

Third-order thinking is noticing the time of day, weather conditions, construction zones, and city events, and deciding not to take that route at all. You are not reacting. You are shaping your course by understanding the broader environment you are moving through.

Most organizations operate and reward at the first order. They prioritize immediate metrics, short-term gains, and fast fixes. A project slips. Add a check-in. A client is unhappy. Offer a discount. A team underperforms. Replace the lead. These are surface-level solutions. *They treat symptoms, not systems.*

A clear example of this shows up in procurement. In many organizations, no one ever gets fired for picking the lowest cost option. On paper, it is easy to defend. But in practice, that kind of decision rarely maximizes value.

Consider hiring a consultant. First-order thinking says to choose the cheapest qualified person who has done something similar before. Second-order thinking says to also look at reputation, experience, or maybe past results. Third-order thinking asks a deeper question. Can this person identify the real problem and solve it? (Does this person bring unique value to the process?)

That is the part most procurement systems completely miss. Some go beyond price and ask for credentials or case studies. But they almost never evaluate the most important factor: The ability to detect and influence human behavior, which shapes every complex challenge. (Consider how many requests for bridges, schools, and airplane components are awarded to the lowest bidder.)

Whether it is project management, legal work, or engineering, outcomes depend on how people think, communicate, and act. Yet I have never seen a procurement process include criteria about emotional intelligence, behavioral insight, or problem diagnosis. They ask what you have done, not how you think. *They hire for capacity, not capability.*

Even more troubling, most clients do not actually know the real problem they are trying to solve. They believe they have already diagnosed it. They just need a body to execute the solution they have already picked. It is like seeing a pothole and deciding to fill it without asking whether the roadbed is collapsing underneath.

So how should you select a consultant?

Start by asking who is highly recommended by people you trust. Referrals matter because they reflect actual experience. Then look for true experts: People who speak, write, are commercially published, and shape thinking in the field. People who have done the work, not just sold the pitch.

But expertise is not enough. Pay attention to how they engage. Real experts listen first. They ask questions. They take time to understand what is happening beneath the surface. They help you cocreate clear objectives and define what success looks like. They work with you to name outcomes, agree on value, and identify the right metrics. And they keep revisiting those metrics to make sure you are making progress toward the right result.

They do not just offer a service. They give you a framework to understand where you are headed, how progress will be measured, and what success will look like when you get there.

That is third-order thinking in action. It moves past the surface and into the system. It avoids the trap of doing the wrong thing efficiently and instead focuses on doing the right thing deliberately.

And let's be honest. You are hiring a consultant because you do not have the expertise yourself. So why waste time pretending to be an expert in *their* field? Why fixate on evaluating their methods with bureaucratic diligence or some artificial sense of procedural rigor when you lack the context to judge it meaningfully? What you care about is whether they can provide the desired outcome. That is the entire point. If they can get you there and show you how you are making progress, then how they do it matters far less than whether it works.

Break Out of Your Mental Echo Chamber

Think about the last time you went to the grocery store. You probably walked the same route you always do. Produce first, then the bakery, then the dairy case. You grabbed the same brand of yogurt, the same cereal, and the same salad dressing. You were not analyzing choices or comparing options. You were on autopilot.

That is the power of unconscious competency, which includes mental shortcuts we rely on to move efficiently through familiar situations. In most cases, they save us time and mental effort. But they can also blind us. When the layout of the store changes or a better option shows up in a different aisle, we miss it. Not because we are careless, but because we are not really thinking. We are just repeating.

We need to be in "conscious competency." We may not think about moving the steering wheel of the car a 10th of an inch frequently to stay in our lane, but we had better be alert to the exit sign when we're on an unfamiliar road on the way to an appointment.

This same pattern shows up in decision making, especially on projects. Unconscious patterns that once helped can start to hurt. When that happens, they turn into cognitive biases. You think you are making a good call, but in reality, your thinking has been distorted.

Some examples of cognitive biases we can see regularly:

Anchoring: Anchoring happens when the first piece of information you receive *becomes the baseline for all future thinking.* On projects, this often shows up during early estimation. The first timeline or budget thrown on the table sets the tone, and even if better data emerges, teams struggle to adjust to the original. That initial number sticks, and decisions are made in relation to it rather than in response to actual needs or evolving complexity. It creates false certainty and locks teams into assumptions that should have been reevaluated.

Confirmation bias: Confirmation bias is the tendency to seek, notice, and favor information that supports your existing beliefs while discounting or ignoring evidence that challenges them. It's especially dangerous in high-stakes or politically charged projects, where leaders may cling to their narrative and selectively interpret feedback or data. Instead of testing ideas, *teams fall into echo chambers.* Good decisions require friction, alternative views, and data that challenge assumptions and don't just reinforce them.

Overconfidence bias: Overconfidence is when people overestimate their own knowledge, skills, and/or ability to predict outcomes. In project settings, this can lead to unrealistic plans, missed risks, and poor contingency strategies. A manager who has "been through this before" may dismiss concerns or gloss over complexity, assuming that experience guarantees success. But every context is different. Confidence should be grounded in awareness, not ego. The most experienced leaders are often the ones who ask the most questions.[3]

Sunk cost: The sunk cost fallacy shows up when people continue investing in a decision, project, or strategy not because it's still the right choice, but because they've already invested so much. "We can't stop now because we've come too far." But money spent, time lost, and effort already poured in are gone regardless. Smart teams know when to walk away, pivot, or pause. Letting go of sunk costs is not failure; it's wisdom. Sticking with a flawed path just to justify past decisions only compounds the damage.

---

[3] For a fascinating example of this, see Walter Isaacson's *Steve Jobs,* Simon & Schuster, 2011, where he terms the trait "reality distortion."

> ## Project Pulse
>
> *The resistance to change because of the ego threat of abandoning the belief in what you have been doing (wrongly) for so long requires coaching, not training, and consequences if changes aren't accepted.*

Scarcity thinking: Scarcity thinking creates a sense of false urgency and pressure. It's the belief that if we don't act now, the opportunity will disappear, or that we must choose the fastest or cheapest path because there are no other options. In practice, this mindset shrinks creativity and drives reactive choices. It leads to hasty vendor selections, poor hires, and rushed launches. Scarcity thinking thrives in environments of fear and overcontrol. The antidote is pausing, zooming out, and creating a wider frame of reference. What's needed is the opposite of scarcity thinking: an abundance mentality.

> *When Pressure Shrinks Your Brain*
>
> There's a moment in *The Dark Knight* when the Joker taunts Batman with a question: "Why so serious?" It's unsettling because we've all been there, trapped in a moment that feels too important to fail. At work, we regularly encounter situations that seem so high-stakes that we abandon the very tools that help us think clearly. We lose our creativity, our ability to challenge assumptions, even our sense of humor. Why? Because we perceive a threat. When that happens, we start operating from the primitive brain. We shift from exploration to protection. From thinking to reacting. Ironically, this is when we need our best thinking the most. Scarcity isn't always about money or time. Sometimes it's just fear wearing a different mask. Use these five questions with your team to bring more awareness into your decision-making process:

Quick bias checklist for teams:

1. What assumption are we treating as fact?
2. What evidence are we ignoring because it does not fit our story?

3. Are we staying the course only because of past investment?
4. Are we mistaking confidence for accuracy?
5. If a new person joined the team today, what would they question first?

These questions take less than 5 minutes. But they can save weeks of missteps. The best teams do not have fewer biases. They are just better at seeing them in time.

Draw Better Maps: How to Navigate Complexity

Mental maps are the internal representations we create to understand the world. They are a blend of beliefs, experiences, frameworks, and assumptions. Everyone has them, *but not everyone updates them.* A map is only useful if it reflects the actual territory of importance to you. When conditions change and the map stays static, you end up making decisions based on outdated patterns. The best leaders update their maps constantly. They don't just learn new facts. They reshape how they see.

"Knowing" isn't enough. We live in a world drowning in data. Dashboards, KPIs, reports, and updates are everywhere. But more data doesn't equal better decisions. The DIKW model—Data, Information, Knowledge, Wisdom—helps us understand why.

At the base is Data: raw, unprocessed facts. By itself, it's noise. When sorted and contextualized, data become Information, something with structure. When information is paired with experience, judgment, and application, it becomes Knowledge. That's where most teams stop. They assume that being informed and experienced is enough.

But the top of the pyramid is Wisdom: knowing which knowledge to apply, when to apply it, and in what way. Wisdom is about perspective, timing, and discernment. It's the rarest layer, and the most valuable.

And yet, society often gets stuck idolizing the lower levels. We reward rote and memorization, standardized tests, and content mastery. We celebrate university degrees and advanced credentials such as PhDs as the pinnacle of human achievement. But those are, at best, markers of accumulated knowledge, not of wisdom. You can meet someone with three degrees and two decades of academic depth, and still find they have no real-world discernment or capacity to navigate nuance. I've lost count of the PhDs I've met who hold extensive data, information, and knowledge in their field, but consistently demonstrate zero wisdom when it comes to applying it!

Most project environments live in the first three tiers. They're optimized for producing reports, validating expertise, and showing you're informed. But they struggle to reach wisdom. Why? *Because wisdom isn't about knowing more. It's about seeing clearly.* It's about recognizing patterns others miss, asking questions others don't, and making choices that align with long-term value, not short-term noise.

Upgrading your mental map means aiming higher than knowledge. It means evolving how you think: from collecting facts to cultivating insight; from reacting to data, to responding with wisdom.

So don't "codify" everything, build universal principles.

In complex environments, codification quickly becomes a trap. It gives the illusion of certainty where none exists. Organizations often try to script answers, procedures, and checklists in pursuit of consistency, but in doing so, they sacrifice adaptability. They confuse memorization with understanding. The result? Teams that can follow instructions but can't think when the situation changes.

Part of the allure is psychological. Codified answers create a *perception* of safety. If you follow the script and something goes wrong, you're not accountable because you were "just following the process." It's a convenient shield against risk and responsibility. But it also kills initiative. It trains people to default to compliance rather than judgment, even when the situation demands something different.

Subject matter expertise reinforces this pattern. We treat experts as people who "know the right answer," instead of those who can navigate ambiguity and make sense of the unknown. But in reality, it's not the answer that matters most; *it's the lens through which you see the problem.* That's what universal principles offer: a durable, transferable way of thinking that travels well between contexts.

Principles like "question your assumptions," "define the problem before solving it," or "optimize for long-term outcomes" are far more useful than memorizing what worked last time. Mental maps built on universal principles don't guarantee perfection. But they equip you to handle the unexpected. They give you something to come back to when your tools stop working, when the data is fuzzy, or when a new variable throws your whole playbook out the window.

Wisdom doesn't come from having a catalog of answers. It comes from developing a philosophy of thinking, one rooted in principles that scale, flex, and adapt. If you want better results, stop asking "What's the right answer?" and start asking "What's the right principle to apply here?" That shift in mindset makes all the difference when navigating complexity.

A friend of mine owns a small, busy restaurant. One day, one of his employees took it upon himself to create a printed table for giving change. It listed all the possible combinations of menu items and the corresponding amounts of change required. The idea was to avoid doing any math at the till. On the surface, it seemed like a helpful gesture, a way to speed things up and eliminate errors.

But the result was the opposite. The table quickly ballooned into a complex, nearly unreadable document. It couldn't possibly cover every scenario. Customers don't always order the same combinations, prices change, and taxes vary. Instead of making things easier, the table introduced friction. The employee would spend time scanning for the "right" answer, slowing down the checkout and creating awkward moments at the register.

What really drove this wasn't efficiency. It was fear. The discomfort of doing mental math, and the anxiety of possibly making a mistake, led to an overengineered solution. Rather than lean into learning a simple skill, the employee built an elaborate crutch. One that ultimately made them all less flexible and more dependent.

It's a perfect example of the illusion of safety that codification offers. If you're using the chart and get something wrong, you can say it wasn't your fault. You followed the system. But that's not how good judgment works. You don't get better by outsourcing your thinking to a chart. You get better by understanding what you're doing and why even if you make a mistake now and then.

In fast-paced, unpredictable environments like restaurants (or projects), the ability to think in real time matters more than rigid rule-following. We need principles, not paperwork. Skills, not scripts. Because the real world doesn't come with a cheat sheet.

Here are some techniques to sharpen your "mental map." Once you commit to thinking more clearly and operating from principles, you need tools to do it. Here are four approaches that help surface better insights, challenge your assumptions, and navigate complexity with more confidence.

Inversion: Instead of asking, "What would make this successful?" ask, "What would cause this to fail?" Inversion forces you to look at risk head-on. It helps you identify blind spots and weak links before they trip you up. It's one of the simplest ways to get to the truth fast by imagining what you'd do if you were trying to sabotage your own effort.

Contrast: Clarity often comes from difference, not detail. What does "good" look like compared to "bad"? How would this decision play out in the short term versus the long term? Use contrast to test your thinking. If you can't articulate the opposite of your position, you probably haven't thought it through well enough. Comparison brings precision.

Ask the why: Don't just gather information—interrogate it. Why are we doing this? Why now? Why this way? Asking "why" repeatedly cuts through noise and helps reveal motives, constraints, and unspoken assumptions. You don't need to be annoying. You just need to stay curious long enough to get past the obvious.

Solve the right problem: One of the most common issues I see in need of correction in organizations is *solving the wrong problem*. People jump to solutions before they've understood what's really going on. The actual issue is often buried beneath an emotional trigger: frustration, fear, and pressure. Until you slow down and name what's underneath, you're just swatting symptoms. Real problem-solving means taking the time to find the root cause, and only then designing corrective action that matters. Otherwise, you're optimizing the wrong thing.

These techniques don't require expertise. They require discipline. Use them regularly, and they become part of how you see the world. Utilize tools that evolve your mental maps toward wisdom, not just information.

Your Two Brains: Fast Instinct Versus Slow Wisdom

Even with the best maps, we're still human. We get emotional. We jump to conclusions. We default to mental shortcuts. If you want to think like a strategist, you need to understand the machinery behind your own mind, and the tension between *fast instinct and slow wisdom*.

Psychologist Daniel Kahneman gave us one of the most useful frameworks for understanding how our minds actually work. He showed that we do not have a single, unified brain running the show. We have two distinct systems, each with its own job.

System 1 is fast, automatic, emotional, and subconscious. This is your *inner survivalist*. It works like a shortcut machine, helping you make snap judgments and react quickly to the world around you. It is the voice in your head that leaps to conclusions without you even realizing it.

System 2 is different. It is deliberate, conscious, and fully present. This is your slow, *reflective self*. It is the part of you that pauses, weighs different possibilities, and looks for a bigger picture beyond the obvious. When you are thinking deeply, solving complex problems, or questioning your own assumptions, you are leaning on System 2.

A good way to see this in action is to picture an elephant and its rider. System 1 is the elephant. It is powerful, emotional, and can move in any direction at any moment. System 2 is the rider trying to steer the elephant. The rider can guide and influence the elephant, but only if they stay aware and know when the elephant is about to bolt.

As a leader, you are not just riding your own elephant. You are helping others steady theirs too. Sometimes you need to help people see that they are even on an elephant in the first place.

Most of the time, System 1 dominates. It is always on, ready to protect you and get you through the day with minimal effort. But that same speed and ease is exactly what can hijack your judgment, especially when the stakes are high. Ironically, the moments when you need clear, thoughtful decision making the most are often the moments when it is hardest to slow down and access System 2.

Mastering this balance is not just about you. It is about understanding how these two systems play out in the people around you. Once you see the elephant, you can learn how to guide it. And once you see the rider, you can help them stay in the saddle when it matters most.

Empathy is one of the most practical ways to "switch" your mind from fast, automatic reactions to deeper, wiser thinking. When you catch yourself quickly labeling someone's behavior as laziness, resistance, or sabotage, you are usually listening to System 1. This quick judgment feels certain and satisfying because it gives you a simple story that explains what is happening. But simple stories are not always true.

If you pause and ask yourself what might be going on for them, you immediately invite System 2 into the room. You shift from blame to curiosity, from certainty to possibility. This small moment of empathy does not just help you understand others more fully; it also stops your own mental autopilot from running the show. You give your brain a chance to see the bigger picture, ask better questions, and respond more thoughtfully.

There are signs you can watch for that show which system is driving you. System 1 shows up as emotional spikes, overconfidence, procrastination, reactivity, and blame. System 2 feels different. It shows up as inquiry, patience, and open-mindedness.

When you notice these signals in yourself or your team, it becomes your chance to flip the switch. Empathy is not weakness. It is one of the strongest tools you have to slow things down, look beneath the surface, and move forward with clarity instead of getting stuck in old stories.

Your team will naturally slip into System 1 thinking from time to time, especially when they are under stress. It is human nature. When people feel pressure or a sense of threat, they cling to mental shortcuts, blame, or quick conclusions because it feels safer in the moment. But when a team stays in this reactive mode too long, problems linger, and real solutions stay hidden.

One of your most important jobs as a leader is to help your people engage their System 2. You do this by asking the kinds of questions that break the cycle of reactivity and open up space for clearer thinking. Simple questions like what we might be missing or what is the real issue here encourage people to pause, reflect, and see more than their first reaction.

When you make this a regular practice, you are not just guiding your team to better answers in the moment. You are building a culture where reflection is valued over reactivity. Over time, you help your people feel safe to slow down, test their assumptions, and tackle problems at a deeper level. This is how you turn a group of individuals into a stronger, thinking team that can handle uncertainty together.

Master strategists do not just analyze more. They notice better. They pause before reacting. They question what others accept. They do not chase speed. They pursue clarity.

And clarity begins with the courage to slow down your thinking, especially when the pressure is on.

In high-stakes environments, the instinct is to accelerate. To solve fast. To act decisively. But the leaders who consistently make better decisions are the ones who resist that reflex. They know that speed without insight is just a faster way to go in the wrong direction.

Slowing down does not mean doing nothing. It means making space. For reflection. For reframing. For inquiry that goes deeper than surface symptoms. It is the discipline of thinking beyond the obvious and the patience to let better answers emerge.

Wisdom is not loud. It does not show up in urgent e-mails or dramatic presentations. It is quiet. Subtle. It whispers things like "Are we solving the right problem?" and "What have we not considered?" It is the voice that helps teams see clearly when others are overwhelmed by noise.

And that is the shift this chapter invites you to make:

- From rushing to reflecting.
- From reacting to responding.
- From being the person with the answer to being the one who asks the question that changes everything.

Because in a world full of complexity, the rarest and most valuable skill is not working harder. It is thinking better.

CHAPTER 6

Perception *Is* Reality (Usually)

There are few things more influential in business than communication, and it goes far beyond the words. Communication is behavior and reveals our underlying beliefs and values. It sets the unwritten rules of what the expected beliefs and values of the team are and drives behavior. Learning to master our own stories allows us to moderate how we "show up." Understanding and influencing others starts with listening. Framing things in terms of someone else's best interests is an essential technique. Communication often breaks down because two parties don't have the ability to hear each other. Project managers need to be able to translate and manage the flow of conversations.

Reframe your stories to change your impact

When I was younger, I had a moment where I realized I wasn't a singular entity, that there was a conversation going on. The best I could describe it, it was like my spiritual and my organic form talking to each other. Before you think I'm crazy, read on, and you might find some familiar settings.

I read *The Untethered Soul*[1] *by Michael Singer* and the author talks about it in terms of a roommate in our head. The roommate can be the biggest bully and critic in some of us if we're not careful.

The roomie gets pretty strong, like someone going to the gym, and it can be hard to overpower this "alter ego." The workout to build up that strength often results from working us over! *We can build up our own*

---

[1] *The Untethered : The Journey Beyond Yourself.* Oakland, CA: New Harbinger Publications.

muscles to change our narrative. The old roomie fades away, and we get a new and better roomie who's respectful and supportive.

This roomie is often "guilt" or "fear" or normative pressures. Roomies whisper in our ear, telling us we can't do things, or the things we have done are woefully insufficient. They are constantly undermining, sometimes without our realizing it.

For some, the roomie is so powerful that there's no defense system in place. The moment a negative story emerges, the roomie convinces us the world is about to end. I remember once preparing for a speaking engagement—after my first trial run, a thought crept in: This talk is going to be terrible. The audience won't get any value from it. It felt like enemy bombers flying in to launch a tactical strike on my psyche.

Earlier in my life, I had no defense against moments like that. Fortunately, by then, I had a strong antiaircraft battery ready. It launched a counterattack within seconds and fended off the incoming assault. That talk ended up being one of the best I've ever delivered. *If I can build these defenses then each one of you can too.*

The Narrative

This is about the dialogue we have with ourselves. For example, one evening our daughter, Marie, jumped off the bed for the first time, while Andie had her back turned. She struck the corner of the nightstand and cut the skin just above her eyebrow. There was blood, plenty of crying, and a flash of fear, followed by Andie snatching up Marie and running out of the room trying to console her (both crying).

After doing a quick diagnostic and confirming there was nothing life-threatening, I could tell Andie was struggling inside. I asked her what was going on, and she got a bit defensive. We've talked about the roomie, and I asked her what her roomie was saying. She admitted things like, "How could you be so stupid?" "You are a terrible mother!" and "You should have been watching!"

I asked her what something positive was that she could tell herself, and she said, "I can't think of anything good to say to myself. I didn't do my best." I said that I knew it was hard to imagine saying something positive and that it was an opportunity to start modelling behaviors for Marie, our 8-month-old daughter, so she develops a healthy roomie.

That gave Andie the courage to lean into the discomfort, leading her to bravely acknowledge that she did her best and that it was a learning experience for all of us.

That reframe mattered. It helped Andie regain perspective and gave her the courage to lean into the discomfort of standing up to her roomie and changing the narrative. She eventually admitted she genuinely did the best she could in that moment. That moment of bravery gave Marie something far more important than a perfect parent. Children do not need flawless protection. They need parents who model what it looks like to meet mistakes with honesty, compassion, and resilience, most importantly for themselves.

Explanatory Style

We have to use positive self-talk in order to produce positive communications to others. For example, "Interception" is my term for catching the roomie in action and intercepting and changing the dialog.

I've experienced personal fear of changing to a positive story. Early in my career, I attended Conversations (Now Crucial Conversations for Mastering Dialogue offered by Crucial Learning) and became aware that we have stories that may not be true; in fact, many of them are fabrications. Sometimes we tell ourselves lies so often that we blend them with reality. This is called "confabulation." You were on the football team, but you didn't start and never made a touchdown catch, except in your retelling of the story.

I remember the moment a few months later when my roomie was trying to be exceptionally negative (a norm when I look back at it), making it scary to even imagine a potential positive outcome in a situation.

It was 2012, and I had just quit my healthy, six-figure corporate job to set out on my own and become an entrepreneur. In hindsight, I wasn't confident enough to do it fully on my own and had been approached by another entrepreneur I had worked with and known for over 10 years. He wanted to partner on a new venture.

It became apparent quickly that we weren't aligned on many things, and conflict flared up. We had each contributed $20,000 to the start-up funds. I woke up one morning to the realization that he had cleaned out the bank account, and my share was gone. In that moment, the wave of intense emotions hit me. Guilt, shame, fear of the future, fear of what I had lost, and fear of letting my family down.

My roomie insisted I was a failure and that there was no hope; nothing positive could come from this situation. I complied as I had learned to do until I remembered my training. I remember talking to myself and saying, what's one positive thing you can think of in this moment? My roomie was an 800-pound gorilla who had gone full tyrant and was slamming around inside my brain. I felt as powerless as a newborn but leaned into it and imagined one small positive thing. I didn't realize it at the time, but that set in motion a life of independence (professionally, personally, and financially) that has allowed me to live the life I wanted to live.

It took a lot of effort to even be open and accepting of a positive outcome. *That was the TSN turning point (I'm originally Canadian; TSN is our ESPN) for me when it came to realizing when I needed to intercept the stories.* I realized later the power of practice and repetition, and how the new stories would get stronger and stronger the more I practiced them. It seems ironic, but we do have to practice the truth and avoid the embellished and fictitious aspects.

During my 2nd year of engineering, one of my professors was discovered to have falsified her credentials. She had used her husband's qualifications to apply for the position and had convinced herself, as well as her colleagues and students, that she was a competent professor of engineering. It's hard to believe that someone could infiltrate an academic institution that many hold to be the pinnacle of society.

We've experienced news anchors and politicians reciting stories of their involvement in gunfire during wars, or emergencies during natural disasters. They've told themselves the embellishments so much that they have confused them with the actual story. This is how, unbelievably, a CEO or university president has to resign after it's discovered that their credentials were falsified, their résumés were inflated, and their awards and accolades unearned.

It's not that they never thought they'd be "found out," it's that they believed the lies embedded with the reality themselves.

News Anchor Brian Williams and Presidential Candidate Hillary Clinton both seemed shocked that their own claimed experiences were proved untrue.

Reframing

The Mona Lisa is one of the most famous paintings in history, known for the penetrating eyes of the subject. But what many people don't realize is that it's the frame that makes the painting so alluring. If the frame were several inches to the left or right, up or down, the effect wouldn't be nearly the same.

The framing is as important as the artistry in many cases. Let's think about changing the perspective of our stories to look at them from a different angle.

When I work with teams, I often ask them to take their hand and put up one finger to represent one story. Then I'd ask them to imagine a different story with another finger and again with another finger. People have such strongly pessimistic stories that they keep going with negative stories finger after finger.

I tell them that hand represents your negative stories. Now raise your other hand, and this is the positive story hand. Give me one positive story. We have to break the "negative default loop."

Why the "loop"? Neural pathways form, which are like habits that become automatic behavior. But, they can be changed by practicing. *They are a complex cocktail of chemicals in our brain that get released based on what we read in our environment and then drive behavior.* They get very strong the more they are practiced and reinforced. We become addicted to them despite them being unhelpful in modern-day life.

We can build new ones the same way. The old ones are never completely gone; they just fade away into the background. But sometimes they pop up unexpectedly. Guilt and shame are typical of those emotions, and these can catch you at any time, unexpectedly. They are powerful emotions that many of us know well, especially me. I have yet to find a useful purpose for either of these emotions in our modern world. They simply hold us back from growth and achieving better outcomes in our lives. Thus, the more we build new habits, the more we can resist the old, negative ones.

People get in the habit of saying "thank you" or "please"; of being tolerant and forgiving; or being resilient instead of resistant and afraid. And the way we speak has a lot to do with that, both in self-talk and in our communications with others.

Words Are Cheap—Behavior Speaks

You can't hide intentions. No matter what words you use, your actions and behaviors will reveal your true intentions. We need to avoid the cognitive dissonance of saying something and then acting in an antithetical manner. Have you ever seen an executive who claims that "customers are our most important asset" but then refuses to speak to them directly?

There is a "scientific" meaning to words and also a "magical" one. "Gay" and "straight" traditionally mean "being happy and carefree" and "moving in a direct line." Today, they are predominantly used to describe sexual orientation.

Moreover, "denotation" is the literal meaning of a word. "Connotation" is that meaning which is imparted in *addition to the literal meaning*. "You require discipline" may mean that you need to better follow the rules, or that you require punishment.

I had a contractor on a project I was managing once, and he was weeks late in pulling together a design with the engineers. He hadn't even asked the client yet about what the requirements for the build would be. I decided to get things started, so I met with the client to develop some initial requirements because I knew the schedule was in trouble. At the next meeting, and with the nicest presence, he went on to start by subtly communicating that the client was at fault for bringing these requirements late and that it may cause some delays, but they would accommodate them as best they could.

I reminded him that the design was in his contract and as such it was incumbent upon them to be leading the design, gathering requirements, and completing a design so they could order things. His presence and language really didn't alter his responsibility. (We hear this all the time in relationship failures: "It's not you, it's me," as if that's supposed to make the breakup easier to live with.)

This is a simple example of what we are actually communicating, regardless of how nicely we deliver it. These factors also matter:

- Tone of voice
- Facial expressions
- Proxemics

- Eye contact
- Cadence
- Volume
- Emphasis
- Intensity

Master the Lost Art of Listening

Meta-listening is the ability to be aware of and assess aspects of one's own auditory perception, essentially "listening to your listening," and using that information to guide behavior or understanding.

Curiosity is the practice of investigating, exploring, and even challenging what you are told. (This is a good way to examine cognitive dissonance.)

"About" questions place things in context and suggest "What about the opposite approach?" or "What about possible competitive reactions?"

Different types of questions are required to determine:

- *Why* something is important, or why you have a certain mission of calling.
- *What* you are trying to accomplish—your goals and objectives.
- *How* you will proceed—your tactics and execution.
- *Where* you will begin and conclude.
- *Who* will be responsible and accountable.

Exercise

In the space below, complete the answers to these questions for a professional or personal project that is important to you now or that you are considering.

Why: _____

What: _____

How: _____

Where: _____

Who: _____

How many of these answers came readily, and which required some thought, or didn't have an answer? Why is that?

Paraphrasing and Other Techniques

To paraphrase is to repeat what you've heard using other words, to test whether you've heard accurately, and to further the conversation expeditiously.

This actually extends the conversation and doesn't delay it. You gain agreement and build trust. Example:

- Speaker: "The most effective way to build consensus is to make it clear that it's something you can live with, not something you'd die for."
- Listener replies: "In other words, we don't have to have a 'win or loss' but rather a compromise we can both support."
- Speaker: "Exactly, so let's examine how to best create it."

This can also be called "testing for understanding" by *asking for the paraphrase*: "Tell me in your words what you believe my point is for you." This will demonstrate whether you've really been understood, and also allow you to calibrate your speed. Most speakers tend to move too *fast without* any measure of comprehension of their remarks. That's the trouble with speeches that are read, church sermons, and many such orations: The speaker has no idea of what the audience truly understands and can apply, only whether they will finish on time or not!

"Labeling", as I use the term, is when you name the story that you believe someone else is playing out with your roomie. It can be really effective if you're right in identifying the story. Even if you aren't, you usually get a second chance to recalibrate and get it right. However, don't do this if you struggle with empathy because you can do a lot of damage if you're not careful.

For example, if you read that the other party in a negotiation is hesitant and you suspect it's because of price, you could say, "it seems like the contract price might be a barrier for you, would that be correct?" You'll either get some version of "that's right" (literally the words, a variation of them, or even a sigh and release of energy). At that point, the other party feels like they've been heard and that you're willing to work with them. You could follow up with, "Based on what you know, why do you think that is?" Labelling takes down defensiveness and opens the door to collaboration and insights that move situations forward.

During negotiations with the contractor discussed previously, he feigned collaboration in solving disagreements by making statements like, "we want this project to be successful for everyone," followed up with comments when he didn't agree with the client's position, such as, "We all just need to get in a room and discuss this like professionals." These are the tools of the passive aggressive to indicate their true thinking and to antagonize you. In this case, somehow insinuating I was acting as less than professional without the courage (or empirical evidence) to suggest it assertively.

But sometimes a label puts things or people in a "drawer" where they seem homogeneous but are really not. Example: "Gen X has the toughest time trying to measure up to the Boomer generation." Maybe some do, but certainly not all. This is why we have so much polarization, because we assume "all Republicans" or "all Democrats" think in certain ways, which is clearly false.

"Mirroring" is a term I use to describe repeating someone else's body language. For example, if someone else crosses their arms, you cross your arms. If they touch their cheek, you touch your cheek. This can build relatedness and take down barriers, whether it's in high-stakes business negotiations or first dates. However, be careful not to overuse it, as it will become blatantly obvious what you're doing.

"Mirroring" can also refer to a technique from neuro-linguistic programming, which suggests you repeat and endorse what you've heard from the speaker. If the recruiter says, "We believe in customers as our most important asset," the candidate says, "Customers are certainly the key resource for any organization" (instead of challenging with, "Aren't your employees your most important resource?"). Mirroring is often as obvious as a ham sandwich, and the other person will feel the listener is simply trying too hard to be accepted or has no original thoughts, or is unwilling to "push back."

Using the active listening techniques, and then summarizing, leads to people saying some version of "that's right" or even an exhale or something that indicates they feel like they've been heard and that you understand. It can also mean "I didn't understand it before, but I do now." Summarization is another technique that allows you to calibrate comprehension and your own speed.

Empirical Evidence

I use this to challenge people's claims and to recognize cognitive dissonance. Often, someone will say they are not good at something, but the evidence shows that you are. "You say you're selling poorly, but you results are in the top three." "Despite all evidence to the contrary, you claim you're unpopular, yet everyone wants to work with you."

There are two key techniques to test the veracity of a statement:

1. What is the evidence?
2. What is the observed behavior?

At that point, you want to "watch your language." If you note someone is late by 10 minutes for every Friday meeting, you don't want to confront them eventually with, "You're not a team player." Use the evidence: "I notice you're late for each Friday meeting by ten minutes, why is that?" (And you'll probably find that child care duties have shifted, requiring some extra time, and you can certainly begin the meeting 10 minutes later instead of alienating an employee with accusations.)

When you use observed behavior and evidence, you can stop telling people what to do. This brings us to the "martial arts of language."[2] The is

---

[2] See the book *The Martial Arts of Language* by Alan Weiss, https://alanweiss .com/shop/books/the-martial-arts-of-language/

means using the other person's momentum in your favor. For example, if someone says:

- You're too young
- You're too old
- You don't know our industry or market
- You live too far away
- You don't have an X degree or certification

You reply: "That's exactly why you need me." Example: "You don't have any experience in the automotive market," you reply, "That's exactly why you need me. You have automotive experts falling from the rafters, but you're all just breathing your own exhaust. You need an expert in service, not in sales."

Ask yourself, "What's in it for me?". This isn't selfish; it's rather a test to obtain your true support and backing (or the other person's). What is the learning like, the challenge, the ability to grow, the referrals, and so forth? This also enables you to find the alignment and reciprocity. You don't have to "control" others' thinking, nor "convert" them, but merely influence it and guide it.

The more questions you ask, the more you'll help other people to learn; that's why interactive professors and teachers are most effective. Self-learning is embraced and remembered far better than rote learning or "founts of knowledge" across the table or in front of the room.

Think about remote versus in-person working arrangements. Many organizations require their staff to be in the office for arbitrary reasons. At best, it's because they don't trust they are productive at home, and at worst, because they have a performance issue, they band-aid fix by demanding they be in the office. By asking yourself and the other party questions and understanding what's in it for each of you, you'll be able to diagnose and address the root cause rather than treating symptoms.

Allow for silences and meditation on the conversation, don't rush to "fill" silences (in which case someone usually says something inane). Use conversations to check your own assumptions to validate or dismiss them and to watch for dissonance, the difference between claims and actions.

Stop Commanding, Start Connecting

We can picture the communication process in this manner:

I Mean --> I Say |----> You Hear > You Get
I Get   I Hear   You Say   You Mean

You can see that there are two fundamental potential problems extant:

1. External interference: There is ambient noise, others present, technological problems, and so forth.
2. Internal interference: There are differing experiences, educations, worldviews, beliefs, and so forth influencing the interpretations psychologically.

Therefore, we have to accept responsibility for ensuring we do our best to lessen the external and internal interference, to use accurate language, and to test for understanding.

Thus:

- Try to create a "what's in it for them" to encourage careful listening and appeal to self-interests.
- Emphasize alignment and not differences. Remember the meaning of true consensus.
- Check your own listening skills, and test to see if you've understood accurately by creating examples and social proof of the points.
- Don't try to "convert" or control, but rather to understand and to influence.
- Ask and converse, don't "tell" or "present."
- Use visuals to share the "mental maps" you may be using. Don't assume people can read your mind or interpret your works consistently accurately.
- Accept silences, don't try to "fill them," which often results in irrelevancies and distraction.

- Never simply assume, ask, "Is this (example) what you mean?"
- Examine dissonance, and ascertain whether words and actions are consistent.

Building Invisible Bridges That Move Mountains

In keeping with the model above, some guidelines for effective bridge building and maintenance.

Don't pursue "right answers." Pursue understanding and agreement, with compromise and consensus as needed. It's a "win/win" proposition, not "win/lose." And be very careful about a "slippery slope": For you to win, the other party doesn't have to "lose"! Accept your positive results graciously and don't bemoan what you might not have achieved.

Always identify your "musts": things you cannot live without. All the rest are "wants," which are negotiable. The problem occurs when we trade away "musts" to preserve "wants,' which is backwards. If you've ever told a realtor, for example, that you must be within a short drive of an excellent school, and they showed you a house 20 miles from one and said, "But look at this views!" you'll know what I mean.

Speak English (or the native language) and not "technoese." It's useless and wasteful to talk in terms of expertise on content (loan defalcations, "the rule of 76," glidepaths, regenerative AI, ACE inhibitors, expansive clay soils, 460cc multi-material driver) if the other party might as well be hearing Swahili or Tagalog.

Project managers are really the "load-bearing" structures for the bridge's strength and durability. That requires careful engineering (attitude, language, compromise, discipline, and accountability).

A bridge requires that you visualize and then create a plan that accommodates each end and ensures a meeting in the middle. There are no compromises about this. Remember that a rocket fired one-tenth degree off the correct course will wind up in a different universe.

In the chart above, work to reduce both external and internal interference. We need to look through others' "lenses" and question our own assumptions and even our own beliefs. And note that the chart must accommodate two-way traffic.

Sympathy is feeling sorry for someone, but empathy is feeling what they feel. It's vital to try to make this adjustment. There are three aspects to empathy that are vital for successful application as shown below in Figure 6.1:

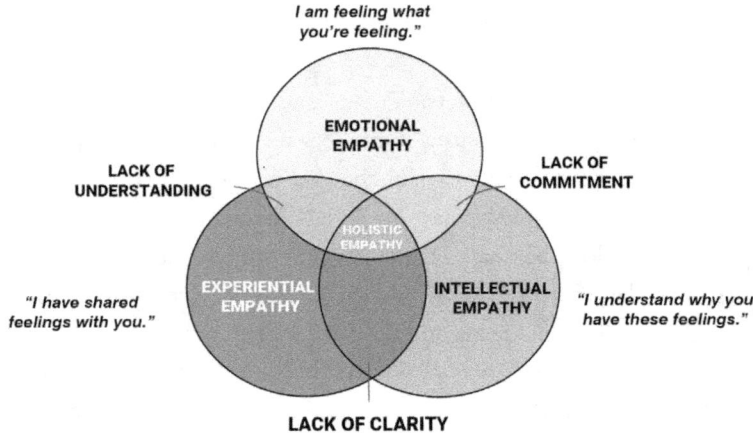

Figure 6.1 Holistic empathy

If you have experiential empathy (you've undergone the issue personally), and intellectual empathy (you understand why the issue is important), but not emotional empathy (feeling what others are feeling), you won't have commitment; if you have emotional empathy but not experiential empathy, you won't be able to relate; and if you have emotional and experiential empathy but not intellectual empathy, you won't be clear on what's needed.

Only with all three conditions will you have "holistic empathy," enabling you to truly understand and help others.

This is not about simply transferring information; it's about creating meaning and commitment, discipline and accountability. Consequently, disagreement and even conflict are healthy and should be used to further progress, not impede it.

Communication is a learned behavior, and you can learn and apply what we've discussed in this chapter. Now, let's turn to how to successfully deal with conflict to create positive outcomes.

CHAPTER 7

Conflict: The Crucible of Greatness—The Opportunity

Where Are We Going or How to Get There: Tension Is Opportunity

Tension is not a warning sign. It is a marker that there is potential for something meaningful underway. It signals that people care. It invites curiosity. When we pause and name the nature of the disagreement, we do not just resolve it. We unlock a deeper level of clarity and trust.

I know you may believe that tension is uncomfortable and want to avoid it. You see it as a wall that's immovable. The key is to stop seeing tension as the "enemy."

What if I told you that every moment of conflict was a doorway with a threshold that can be crossed to build trust, respect, and a safer environment? High-performing teams get curious instead of avoiding the tension.

The most effective leaders know that Tension is a sign of engagement:

- When someone challenges a decision or resists a path forward, it may not be defiance; it may be devotion. They're "leaning in." They're emotionally invested.
- Apathy is easy to miss because it's quiet. But tension is loud. And that's a gift. It tells us there's something at stake worth caring about.
- They see the hidden door in the wall, open it, and show the team how to step through it. Your role is to guide your team through the conflict, not get in the box with them.
- It builds ownership.

- It builds a culture of accountability because team members are responsible for problem-solving instead of "mom" or "dad" getting in to pass judgment and direct traffic
- It grows the team emotionally and in critical thinking

Figure 7.1 illustrates the framework.

Are We Fighting About "Where" or "How"?

Sometimes teams *think* they're disagreeing about method, but they're actually misaligned on vision. Or vice versa. That's why your role as a

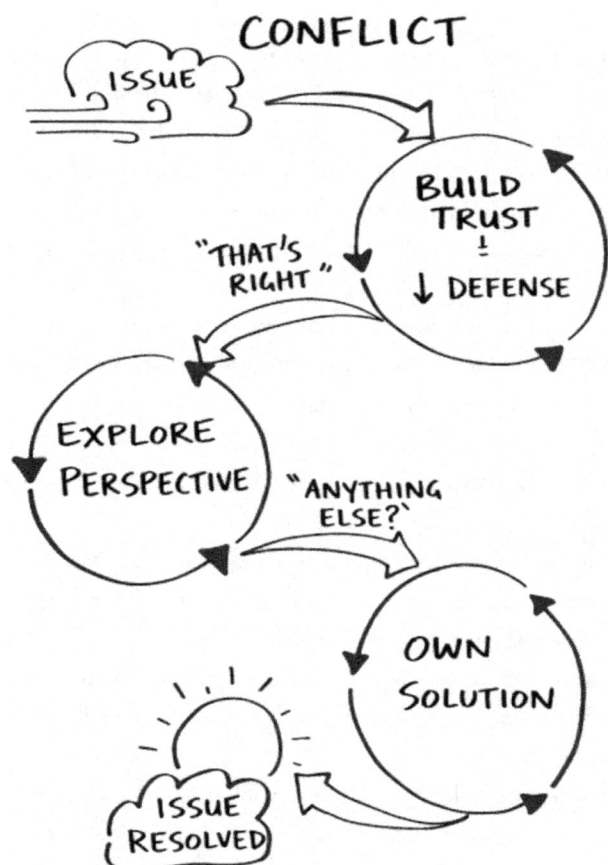

Figure 7.1 Conflict framework

leader or facilitator is to listen for the real layer of disagreement and bring it into the open.

Imagine a team of explorers setting off on a canoe journey into the wilderness. Their destination is clear. They are heading toward a remote village at the far end of a winding river. The group is aligned on purpose, committed to the goal, and eager to begin.

But within hours, tension surfaces.

One group wants to stick to the shoreline. "We should move cautiously," they say, "and scout every bend, avoid unnecessary risk." They value precision and control.

The other group urges a faster pace. "We are losing time. Trust the current. We can adjust as we go." They value momentum and adaptability.

Neither group is wrong. But they are locked in disagreement. Paddles pause mid-stroke. Tones sharpen. Frustration simmers. Someone mutters, "Maybe we are not on the same page after all."

This is a turning point.

Not because the team disagrees, but because they are caught in a moment of unspoken tension. If ignored or mishandled, it could erode trust and fragment the team. But if engaged skillfully, this moment holds something else, a chance to get stronger.

So they pull off to the riverbank.

Project Pulse

Conflict is almost always about either destinations or means to reach them. Each requires a different resolution technique.

They pause. They talk. Not about the route, but about what matters to each of them. What they are trying to protect. What they are afraid to lose. As they listen, the mood shifts. They stop arguing about paddling strategies and start seeing each other more clearly.

By taking time to understand where each other is "coming from," they realize something surprising. They are not opposed, but they are holding different pieces of the same truth. One side brings stability. The other brings speed. And together, they design a better way to travel, one that neither group would have created on their own.

This is what tension offers: The ability to compromise on something even better.

It is not just something to survive. It is a source of insight, alignment, and creativity. When people feel safe enough to stay in the conversation, when they are equipped with the right tools and mindset, tension becomes the moment a team moves from individual effort to collective strength.

Just like in the river expedition's remote village, the destination in the project world needs to be clear. It needs to be described in terms of objectives and outcomes with metrics to measure progress toward them along the way. It could be reduced employee turnover, leading to lower cost of recruitment, measured by the monthly turnover rate and absolute recruitment costs.

Story: Anxiety Loves a Plan (But That's Not Leadership)

This was "one of those projects." It was complex, transformational, and already exhausting for everyone involved. There had been months of staff turnover with constant struggles to recruit the right leads and real subject matter experts. Despite everyone's best efforts, the project had slipped behind schedule.

Things came to a head when a critical stakeholder session fell flat. Instead of bringing people together, it left the team frustrated and uncertain. I knew moments like this could become tinderboxes. Anxious sponsors want to act fast. They want to feel like they are doing something to fix the mess. My role as an advisor was to help the sponsor keep things steady and not overreact. But his anxiety took hold, and he did exactly what I had hoped to prevent.

He focused on what she believed was the obvious problem. In his mind, the root cause was clear. He decided the project manager did not have a work plan. He compared this project to another one he often held up as the model project. He said they had their entire plan laid out in detail on software, and that was why they had been so successful. He did not stop there and unloaded every frustration he had been carrying, blaming the project manager for not having a plan, not communicating properly, and for other gaps he had been stewing on for months. His solution was just as clear. Build the work plan, and everything would get back on track.

I let him say everything he needed to say and did not push back. I listened carefully to what was underneath the frustration so I could understand where his idea of the fix was coming from. When he finished, I paraphrased what I had heard to show I understood. When he let out a sigh confirming he felt heard, I reminded him that the team already did have a detailed work plan in the chosen software. They even had a Microsoft Project file built out. They also used a high-level summary in Mural software every day. The structure he was demanding already existed and had been in place for quite some time.

That changed the conversation. I pointed out that if the plan were there, then the real issue could not be that it did not exist. The real gap was ownership. The new lead had not picked up the plan and made it his own. They were not using it to guide the work the way the previous lead had done. It was not a planning problem. It was a people problem.

In that moment, there was tension. His fix was neat and clear in his mind and gave a sense of control. Letting go of that was not easy. We sat in that discomfort together and worked through it. Slowly, he saw that his thinking was flawed. We needed to shift his energy from blaming and demanding a new plan to supporting the new lead so they could step up and own what was already there.

That was the moment we moved from disagreeing on what to do to aligning on what would really work. It reminded me that when people are under pressure, they reach for what feels simple. But leadership means staying with the mess long enough to see what is true and choosing the right fix, even when it is not comfortable.

Questions to ask to diagnose these issues:

- "What does success look like?"
- How will we know when we've arrived?
- What metrics will we use to measure our progress along the way?

If the end point is not clear, then build alignment on a shared picture of where you're going. If the end point is clear, then check for alignment on how.

- What's the best path forward from here?
- What do you see as the next steps?
- What assumptions have we made on what to do or how to do it?
- If the how is not clear, then explore ways forward and build alignment on how to get there.

Lessons From the Blind Men and the Elephant

An ancient story tells of several blind men who were asked to describe an elephant by touch. One felt the trunk and insisted that an elephant was like a snake. Another held the leg and argued that it was like a tree. A third touched the ear and declared that it was like a fan. Each man was convinced of his truth, yet each truth was partial. They were correct in what they observed and mistaken in assuming their perspective was complete.

Conflict in teams often follows the same pattern. Each person sees a problem, a decision, or a relationship from a particular vantage point. When another person describes the same situation differently, it appears as opposition. In reality, it is rarely opposition. More often, it is simply the same reality seen through a different lens. What feels like conflict is usually a collection of partial truths pressing against each other.

When we begin to understand that every perspective grows out of a unique experience, knowledge, and position, the tension changes. The certainty of who is right gives way to curiosity about what others are seeing. When the tree, the snake, the fan, and the spear are combined, the full elephant appears. In the same way, diverse perspectives enrich the understanding of the whole picture.

The true obstacle is not disagreement but the belief that one view is the entire truth. The moment we hold our perspective as the complete story, we limit ourselves and close the door to learning. The moment we listen to others not as opponents but as contributors, we discover clarity that no single view could provide on its own.

Project Pulse

Most conflict is not opposition; it is perspective. What feels like resistance is often someone holding another part of the truth.

Listening Your Way Out of Gridlock

There is a well-known story in leadership circles called the Abilene Paradox:

A family is sitting on a porch in Coleman, Texas, on an unbearably hot afternoon. The sun is high, the air is still, and no one is eager to move. Then someone suggests, almost casually, that they drive to Abilene for dinner. It is a 70-mile trip through dry, dusty roads in a car with no air conditioning. No one is enthusiastic about the idea, but one person agrees, assuming the others are interested. The next person goes along for the same reason. One by one, each family member consents, not out of genuine desire, but to keep the peace and avoid being the one who says no.

They make the trip. The food is bad. The heat is unbearable. The entire experience is draining. When they return home, someone finally says, I did not actually want to go. Everyone else admits the same thing. They all agreed to something none of them wanted, each assuming the others were on board.

This is the heart of the Abilene Paradox. It is not a story about disagreement. It is a story about people failing to speak their truth. It is a story about false consensus that forms when individuals withhold their honest views to avoid tension or rejection. What results is not alignment, but quiet resentment, confusion, and disengagement.

Project Pulse

Steven Gaffney, an expert on honesty who advises executives, has *said*, "It's not about what people say, it's about what *they don't say*."

You probably know this dynamic all too well. It might have happened at a restaurant, during a project meeting, or around a boardroom table.

You nodded along. So did everyone else. Something felt off, but no one said anything. Later, the team executed on a plan no one fully believed in. The group did not fall apart because of conflict. It stalled because of the silence.

Breaking the Abilene cycle requires more than asking for input. It requires "listening" for what people are holding back. It requires making it safe for someone to say, I am not comfortable with this, without fear of being seen as difficult, negative, or disloyal.

You can say:

- I would rather hear your real opinion than have false agreement.
- Is there anything about this that feels off to you?
- Just because we are quiet does not mean we are aligned. Let us check.

The real test is not whether people agree. It is whether they feel free not to.

And here is the surprising part: When someone finally says what everyone else is thinking, it usually breaks the tension, not the trust. Someone laughs. Another person says, thank you. The conversation opens. People start telling the truth. And that truth becomes the foundation for forward movement.

When someone finally says, that is exactly what I have been feeling, that is your signal. Not just that you have created clarity, but that you have restored connection.

And maybe, if you are lucky, someone in the room will smile and say, I guess we do not need to go to Abilene after all.

Find the Hidden Third Path No One Sees (Yet)

When teams are locked in a dead-end debate between two opposing choices, a surprising third option often emerges, but only if you hold the tension long enough to see it. It's not a forced compromise or a bland middle ground; it's a fundamentally different way of seeing the problem that changes what's possible.

It often comes from being willing to zoom back out, to examine what we are not seeing and what if there's a better solution here? This builds ownership because everyone contributed through the process of its creation. Thus, conversation becomes bigger and better, with higher value, and often much more creative and innovative.

This pursuit shines a light on leaders' blind spots, because leaders can't see everything,

Who are we as leaders to assume that we have the best answer? Why not let the team work through the conflict and see what emerges? If your option is still better, you can still pursue it. If you begin with it, however, you bypass the value that emerges from conflict, such as learning critical thinking skills, building an understanding of each other to strengthen relationships, and normalizing experimentation and risk taking, and you "condition" people to do what they are told with minimum compliance.

The magic happens when you leave the conflict with people firmly behind the direction. True alignment and ownership are not just nodding heads in a meeting. They show up in the words people use, the actions they take, and the way they take responsibility when things get messy.

That means people will speak about the direction as *ours*, not *yours* or *theirs*. There is clear agreement on the goal and the path. You see people moving in the same direction without second-guessing every step.

It feels as if there is a sense of relief, clarity, and sometimes renewed energy. People stop picking apart the plan and start asking, "What do we need to do to make this real?" You notice people leaning in instead of pulling back.

It sounds like "commitment words." "I will…" instead of "Someone should…." You hear questions about next steps, timelines, and ownership, not blame or excuses.

Test for alignment: Ask people "what" or "how" questions to test for understanding and actions. Listen for gaps or different interpretations. Ask, "What worries you about this?" to surface any unspoken resistance. If you hear hesitation, do not ignore it. Circle back and address it:

- If still not aligned, circle back.
- If aligned, confirm next steps. Before you leave the room, confirm who owns what, what happens next, and when. Agree on how you will check progress together.

- Establish what the ownership will look like after the discussion: The people closest to the work hold the pen. They make the plan theirs. You do not have to keep pushing it from above because they carry it forward themselves. When things slip, they step in early instead of waiting to be told.

This will all enable you to "light up" innovation, before it's too late to do so.

CHAPTER 8

Ignite Innovation Before It's Too Late

Projects by nature are creating value by achieving a new future state, and that is impossible without some level of innovation. Strong innovation muscles come from certain underlying beliefs and values, an environment that can be created. Innovation is the antithesis of perfectionism. It comes from the ability to continue to move forward through the fog and through experiments. New ideas come from friction, so conflict needs to be embraced, not avoided.

Innovation Starts With Environment, not Brilliance

With the pace of change in the world today, unlocking innovation is no longer a nicety. It is a fundamental requirement for any organization that wants to stay relevant and resilient into the future. The old model of making products you tell people they want, like General Motors did for decades, simply does not work anymore. Customers want more than basic utility. They expect their problems solved in ways that delight them, with an experience that feels effortless, human, and worth sharing. If your organization cannot deliver that, someone else will. And if you do not reposition yourself to help make this possible for your clients or the organization you work for, then you are already on your way to being obsolete too.

Case Study: Nokia: When Lack of Innovation Kills a Giant

In the early 2000s, Nokia was the world's dominant mobile phone manufacturer, commanding over 40 percent global market share. It was a national pride in Finland, a technological pioneer, and widely admired for its hardware excellence, supply chain efficiency, and brand recognition.

But within less than a decade, Nokia's phone business was sold to Microsoft for a fraction of its former value. What happened?

Nokia wasn't technologically behind. Internally, it had already prototyped touchscreen phones, explored app ecosystems, and built early versions of what would later resemble smartphone operating systems. Nokia engineers knew the future was software-centric, and some even proposed models that resembled Apple's iPhone years before it launched. In many ways, Nokia saw the future but couldn't act on it.

What held Nokia back was a lack of delivering on innovation because of a toxic internal culture. Research by Harvard Business School and INSEAD uncovered that fear was the dominant emotion inside Nokia during this crucial period. Leaders feared telling the truth. Mid-level managers feared giving bad news to superiors. Product teams feared experimenting too far from the core. The game-changing ideas were there, but they could never move forward to successful implementation because of the environment.

Nokia's culture had become risk averse, hierarchical, and politically charged. Bold ideas were met with skepticism or buried. Dissent was seen as disloyalty. Rather than innovate, teams optimized. Rather than disrupt themselves, they protected status and structure. As one insider put it, "We were a hardware company pretending to be a software company; pretending everything was fine."

When Apple launched the iPhone in 2007, Nokia dismissed it publicly as a niche product. Internally, they panicked, but it was too late. Apple and Android leapfrogged Nokia by creating seamless ecosystems of hardware, software, and services. Nokia tried to catch up, but its fragmented software strategy (Symbian, Maemo, MeeGo, and Windows Phone) failed to gain traction.

By 2013, Nokia had fallen so far behind that it sold its handset business to Microsoft, a deal that ultimately failed and was written down as a multibillion-dollar loss. A company once worth over $200 billion was dismantled because it couldn't align culture with strategy. What is it costing you to have those ideas right there with no way for them to break through?

When we picture innovation, we often default to dramatic moments of genius. Steve Jobs unveiling the iPhone. Elon Musk launching rockets. Einstein scribbling equations on a chalkboard. But the reality is far more grounded. Innovation rarely begins with brilliance. It begins with environment.

The best ideas do not emerge fully formed. They grow through experimentation, friction, and feedback. But only when people feel safe enough to explore without needing every move to be right the first time. Innovation is not about flawless plans. It is about creating the conditions for forward movement even when the outcome is uncertain.

People are certainly entitled to their own beliefs and values. But once you step into leadership, your beliefs are not just personal anymore. They shape the experience of everyone around you. Your responsibility is to shape a team environment that unlocks the best of your team and their ability to innovate.

Leadership is not a free space for unfiltered personal values. It is a professional discipline. Just like an accountant needs financial expertise and a lawyer needs legal fluency, a leader needs beliefs that are useful for leading people. Your thinking becomes the operating system your team runs on.

Some beliefs open up possibilities. Others quietly shut it down. If you believe people are lazy, you will lead with pressure and control. If you believe people want to contribute, you will lead with trust and challenge.

You have taken on the responsibility of guiding human beings. That means upgrading your internal world to match the weight of that responsibility. You do not need to be perfect, but you do need to be intentional. Ask yourself. Are my beliefs helping the people I lead grow, or are they protecting my comfort at their expense? How are my beliefs enhancing or limiting my team's innovation?

Model the behavior you seek, especially in the most difficult moments.

Anyone can model values when things are easy. The real test is how you show up when things go sideways. When someone disappoints you. When the pressure is high. When the outcome is unclear.

If you collapse into fear or overcontrol, your team learns to play it safe. If you stay grounded and keep listening, they learn that courage is allowed here.

You do not need to give a speech about innovation. You need to show what it looks like to stay present when the outcome is uncertain. Your behavior sets the tone. Your nervous system teaches them what is safe.

You are not just leading the work. You are shaping the environment that the work lives in. The environment you create through the behaviors you model is the strongest predictor of what your team will create in return.

There are basically three kinds of innovation.

1. Opportunism occurs when, in the moment, you are "triggered" to take advantage of an event or circumstance. You might see an earlier plane delayed that may get you to your destination much faster than your later reservation.
2. Conformist innovation occurs when we make an existing product or service far better. Uber is really a taxi service, but with high technology, English-fluent drivers, and immaculate vehicles.
3. Nonconformist innovation occurs when you create something brand new and not before done. Amazon is the poster child for this (it started out as a bookseller). Ask yourself why the innovative Sears Roebuck, selling items via catalog and trains in the late 19th century, didn't morph into Amazon. The reason is that they focused on profits and didn't prize or reward innovation.

Once the culture is calibrated, your team needs structure. Innovation cannot rely on mood or magic. It needs tools and processes in repeatable forms that help people recognize what kind of innovation they are driving.

Not all innovations look the same, and not every moment calls for disruption. Sometimes what is needed is not reinvention, but adaptation of something proven in one environment to another. Sometimes it is bold defiance. And sometimes it is quick action when a door opens unexpectedly.

Refer to The *Innovation Formula* by Alan Weiss and Michel Robert.

Progress Beats Perfection Every Time

Trying to get everything right before you move is a death sentence for innovation. Progress does not require perfect clarity. It requires movement. Especially in today's pace of change, where the map keeps shifting, *and the cost of waiting is higher than the cost of trying.*

Sometimes you have to fix the plane after you are already in the air, falling toward the ground!

Perfection is not just a standard. It is a belief system. It whispers that unless the conditions are ideal, nothing should begin. That belief feeds emotional hesitation. It creates delay and more often than not, it means nothing gets shipped.

But innovation lives in motion. It feeds on feedback. You do not get to great by standing still.

James Dyson did not invent the first vacuum cleaner. He was not a billionaire with a global team. He was a frustrated engineer who believed vacuums could work better. Traditional models lost suction and clogged constantly. He thought he could fix that.

So he began. The first prototype failed. So did the second. Then the 10th. Then the 100th. Most people would have stopped long before that. Dyson did not. He kept going until he built prototype number 5,127. That was the one that finally worked.

That number is not just about persistence. It is a reminder that perfection is not the point. Dyson did not succeed because he was a genius. He succeeded because he created an environment where learning was the measure of progress. Each prototype was a conversation with the problem. A way to understand it better.

Innovation happens when the environment gives people permission to keep moving forward even when success is not guaranteed. Dyson's story is not about brilliance. It is about resilience. The outcome was new technology, but the real innovation was the mindset that said, "just keep going."

Innovation does not solely depend on bursts of inspiration or dramatic turning points. Instead, they emerge through focused direction, thoughtful action, and sustained effort over time. The most meaningful breakthroughs are not born from intensity. They are the result of steady, deliberate movement aligned with a clear sense of purpose.

The visual model illustrates this with clarity. It shows that true success depends on the intersection of three elements: desire, action, and consistency. Each one plays a vital role. When all three come together, forward motion becomes sustainable and meaningful. But when one is missing, the entire system breaks down. Each absence creates a specific kind of failure. You can see this in Figure 8.1.

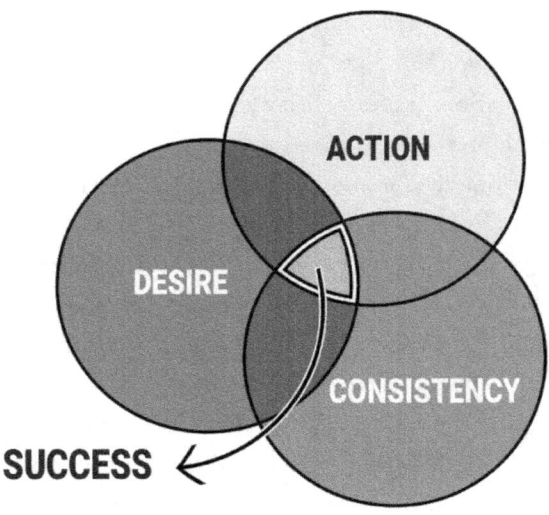

Figure 8.1 Success interaction

When you have desire and discipline but lack action, you fall into the dreamer's limbo. You have the internal drive and a clear structure for how to move forward, but you remain stuck. Nothing changes because nothing is initiated. The vision stays trapped in the realm of potential, never tested, and never real.

When you have action and discipline but no desire, you end up in the empty grind. You keep moving, and you stay consistent, but you feel disconnected from the work. There is no deeper "why," no internal resonance. Your efforts become mechanical and joyless, and over time, that emptiness wears you down. (This may be the grind of a 9-to-5 job.)

When you have action and desire without discipline, you live on the rollercoaster ride. You are excited. You are busy. You are full of ideas and momentum, but without structure and follow-through, your progress becomes unpredictable. You lurch forward in bursts, only to lose steam and stall. The cycle repeats, and over time, the inconsistency erodes your confidence.

Successful innovation is found not in any one element alone, but in the space where all three meet. It begins with knowing what matters to you. It deepens when you take action aligned with that purpose, and it becomes real when that action is repeated over time with care, intention, and focus.

This is what discipline really means. Not rigidity, not control, but the steady return to what matters, practiced often enough to produce something lasting. Innovation does not require drama. It requires rhythm, structure, and the willingness to stay with the work long enough to let something extraordinary take shape.

When innovation is working, it generates momentum. People begin to contribute new ideas, possibilities expand, and confidence grows, but without a clear process for evaluation, creative energy can quickly become scattered. Instead of progress, you are left with distraction. Instead of clarity, you end up with noise. Ideas start pulling in different directions, and the team loses its sense of focus. The goal is not to follow every possibility. The goal is to stay oriented and move toward what matters.

In order to do that, you need discernment. *Innovation will always bring more options than capacity.* Without a way to assess what comes up, it becomes easy to chase volume over value. The best innovators are not those who generate the most ideas, although numbers do help. They are the ones who consistently recognize which ideas are worth pursuing and which ones are not.

Project Pulse

Innovation is like gold: You have to mine it with scrutiny, finding false trails, then some success, then "pure gold."

To support that clarity, use a simple set of questions. These will help you evaluate whether an idea contributes to your desired outcome or pulls you away from it.

1. **Does this move us closer to our intended outcome?**
   If the answer is unclear, slow down. Innovation should always serve a meaningful direction. An idea that seems interesting but does not connect to your goal is likely a distraction.
2. **Is this solving a meaningful problem, or just an easy one?**
   Some ideas feel rewarding because they are simple to execute. But convenience is not the same as value. Direct your attention toward ideas that address the problems that matter most.

3. **Can we test this with minimal risk?**

   A good idea often begins as a small experiment. If it cannot be tested quickly, ask whether it is the right idea for this stage. Learning does not require full commitment. It requires contact with reality.

4. **What trade-offs does this require?**

   Every yes comes with a cost. Time, energy, and attention are finite. Be clear about what you are choosing not to do in order to say yes to this idea.

5. **Does this strengthen or dilute our identity?**

   True innovation brings you into closer alignment with who you are. If an idea stretches your values or creates confusion about your purpose, it may not belong in the process.

These questions are not meant to create hesitation. They are meant to create focus. When you apply them consistently, they protect your attention, guide your choices, and keep the process aligned with what matters.

Tiny Experiments = Big Breakthroughs

Innovation begins by changing how you think, and the biggest barrier to that change is often the set of assumptions you do not even realize you are carrying. These invisible patterns shape your decisions, your interactions, and the way you respond to challenges. If you want different results, you need to start by seeing differently and that begins with small, deliberate experiments.

These are not grand gestures. They are subtle, intentional choices that disrupt your usual habits. It might mean speaking in a meeting when you would normally hold back. It could be asking a clarifying question instead of pretending you understand. It might be offering a bold idea, even if you are afraid someone will dismiss it. These small actions test the edges of your comfort zone. They create new data, and over time, they reshape your thinking.

Thinking drives decisions. Decisions drive behavior, and behavior drives outcomes. That is the chain. If you want new outcomes, it begins with choosing a different response in a moment that matters. You do not need to overhaul everything; you just need to try one new thing, observe what happens, and let that feedback guide your next move.

"Insanity is doing the same thing over and over again and expecting different results." (Unknown, although it's often attributed to Einstein)

These small risks matter more than they seem. They build the muscle of innovation. They shift your posture from passive to engaged, and they teach your nervous system that experimenting is not dangerous. It is how learning happens.

The same principle applies to innovation in the work itself. Breakthrough products do not emerge fully formed. They are the result of a long series of small, deliberate choices. Each prototype, each draft, each round of feedback represents a tangible expression of thinking. The goal is not to get everything right on the first attempt. The goal is to keep moving the idea forward.

Whether you are refining a service, launching a new offer, or building a product from the ground up, meaningful innovation comes from momentum. You take the next clear step, observe what it teaches you, make adjustments, and continue. Over time, these small decisions compound into something meaningful and valuable.

One example of this approach comes from the early days of Instagram. When founders Kevin Systrom and Mike Krieger first launched their app, it was not the polished platform we know today. It began as a completely different product called Burbn, a location-based check-in app that included photo sharing as just one feature among many.

As they watched how users interacted with the app, they noticed a clear pattern. People were not using the check-in features. They were not interested in badges or location tracking. But they were sharing photos. Over and over again. That one simple behavior stood out.

Instead of pushing forward with their original vision, Systrom and Krieger made a choice. They stripped the product down to its core. All the clutter was removed, and they focused entirely on photo sharing with filters. The result was Instagram.

It was not a dramatic pivot in a single moment. It was the product of close listening, thoughtful simplification, and the willingness to act on a small but consistent signal. By following what was already working and having the discipline to let go of the rest, they created a product that quickly grew from a few thousand users to over a million in just a matter of months.

Innovation in this case did not come from a big reveal or a perfect plan. It came from a series of clear, measured steps based on what users were showing them. Each decision was guided by feedback. Each change was an experiment. The final product emerged not through luck or brilliance, but through attention, focus, and small adjustments made with care.

This is how real innovation takes shape. It does not require grand gestures or flawless execution. It requires consistent effort, thoughtful iteration, and the willingness to remain engaged in the process even when the result is still unclear. That is what allows ideas to grow. That is what turns potential into progress. And that is how innovation becomes not just possible, but repeatable.

How friction fuels innovation (and why that's good)

We often think of friction as a problem, in and of itself, to be solved. Something to "smooth out." Something that gets in the way of flow. But in reality, friction is a necessary part of any system that produces something new. Without friction, nothing changes. Without challenge, there is no refinement: If there's no heat, there's no light.

Friction, when guided well, becomes the spark that transforms ideas into something stronger. It is how diverse perspectives collide, test each other, and shape a more complete view of what is possible. It is not comfort that drives innovation. It is the discomfort of having your thinking challenged, your blind spots exposed, and your assumptions reexamined in the presence of others.

Healthy innovative cultures do not eliminate friction. They build containers for it. They create conditions where disagreement is welcomed and where critical thinking is not just allowed but expected. The goal is not to prevent tension. *The goal is to direct it.* Friction becomes fuel when it happens inside an environment of trust, shared purpose, and psychological safety.

When people with different backgrounds, views, and ways of thinking come together, friction is inevitable. But that is also where the best ideas come from. Innovation does not thrive in rooms where everyone agrees. It thrives in rooms where people are willing to question, challenge, and explore ideas that are not yet fully formed.

You can think of it as "constructive collision." Each perspective brings its own shape. When those shapes bump into each other, something new is revealed. That only happens when people are willing to listen, speak honestly, and stay engaged even when it is uncomfortable.

One of the clearest examples of this comes from Pixar. Their most valuable creative process is something they call the "Braintrust." It is a group of filmmakers, writers, and animators who gather during the development of every major film. The group's role is not to approve or reject work. It is to challenge it. They ask hard questions. They point out what is not working. They bring the truth, even when it is uncomfortable.

What makes the Braintrust powerful is not just the feedback itself. It is the environment. Everyone in the room shares the same goal: to make the story better. There is no hierarchy in the conversation. Directors do not have to accept the feedback, but they do have to hear it. The result is a space where ideas are tested rigorously, but without ego or defensiveness. That friction produces stories that resonate deeply and perform consistently at the highest level.

If you want innovation to grow inside your team or organization, you have to normalize friction. Not all conflicts are destructive. When people trust one another, care about the outcome, and are invited to bring their full thinking to the table, disagreement becomes a gift. It forces clarity. It deepens understanding. And it makes the final result stronger than what any one person could have created alone.

The absence of friction is not harmony. It is often silence. It is disengagement, and it is a warning sign that people no longer believe their voice matters.

Innovation is not created by smoothing out every edge. It is created by inviting the edges to meet with purpose and care.

Conflict Breeds Innovation (or Vice Versa?)

Conflict is often misunderstood. It is not the enemy of progress. It is a catalyst for clarity. When conflict shows up, it usually means something important is at stake. People care, they are invested, and they are seeing the problem from different angles. That tension is not something to avoid. It is something to engage with skill and purpose.

If friction is the spark, then conflict is the heat. It is what happens when ideas collide with force, when assumptions are challenged directly, and when emotions rise in the room. The presence of conflict does not mean something is wrong. It often means something real is trying to emerge. The challenge is not how to prevent conflict. The challenge is how to hold it in a way that leads to learning instead of damage.

Avoiding conflict may feel like keeping the peace, but it often delays the very clarity a team needs. Unspoken tension creates confusion. Resentment builds. Alignment breaks down. The better move is to stay in the heat. Stay open, stay curious, and stay committed to the shared goal, even when emotions run high.

Innovation thrives in environments where hard conversations are welcomed. The presence of conflict is not a sign that something is broken. It is often a sign that something important is trying to come to the surface. Your job is not to suppress it. Your job is to hold the space so it can do its work.

CHAPTER 9

Silent Killers of Project Success (And How to Beat Them)

There are maladapted behaviors that serve the sufferer in the moment to the detriment of project objectives and themselves. Normalizing these behaviors degrades team performance. We must identify and deal with these behaviors in order to understand what is expected from the role and when someone is not a fit.

Slaying Procrastination Before It Strangles Results

Procrastination is not a time management issue. It is a fear issue. I have seen it more often than any other pattern in building high-performance teams, and it shows up in people who are intelligent, capable, and driven. That is what makes it so sneaky. When someone smart is stuck, we often assume they are being strategic, busy with something else, or taking time to get it right. But in reality, they are caught in a loop of emotional avoidance.

At its core, procrastination is a failure of emotional regulation. The brain senses a threat to competence, credibility, belonging, or control, and responds by avoiding the task altogether. It is not laziness, it is self-protection, and unless you address the emotional layer underneath, no amount of task lists or nudges will move the needle.

There are only three real levers. You can reduce the threat. You can increase the perceived reward. Or, if there are no other options, you can increase the fear. But that last one comes with a cost. Pressure can force short-term action, but the moment the pressure disappears, the behavior disappears with it. It becomes a pattern of dependency rather than growth.

This is why psychologically safe environments matter. They are not soft skills. They are the execution infrastructure. When people feel safe enough to risk imperfection, they stop avoiding and start engaging. The small things get addressed early. The tough things move forward. Teams gain momentum because people are no longer spending their energy managing fear.

Procrastination strangles progress quietly. It looks like waiting for more data. It sounds like someone saying they just need more time to polish the slide deck. It feels like inertia, but underneath it all is fear. Fear of failing. Fear of being exposed. Fear of not being enough.

Your job is to name it, not shame it. Bring it into the light. Help people shrink the threat or expand their sense of clarity, meaning, or agency. Create the space for action to become safe again because when fear loses its grip, movement almost always follows.

Dealing With the Duckers and Dodgers

Emotional discomfort is one of the most underestimated forces in project work. When the stakes are high and the pressure kicks in, people don't always lean in. Sometimes they slide sideways. They avoid, deflect, delay, or delegate without ever saying so out loud. They do not come right out and say, "I do not want to own this." Instead, they engage in a subtle, often well-practiced set of behaviors that allow them to stay close enough to the work to appear engaged, while distancing themselves from the risk that comes with real responsibility.

Team dynamics are an intricate dance. In healthy teams, that dance is built on shared purpose, clarity of roles, and mutual accountability. But when fear creeps in, the dance can become evasive. People start to side-step hard conversations. They look busy without being productive. They default to consensus even when clarity is needed. They may even weaponize vulnerability, leaning on emotion as a way to opt out of leadership moments without ever appearing to do so.

You cannot lead well if you cannot see this pattern, and once you see it, you cannot pretend it is something else.

Ducking and dodging rarely look like outright refusal. They look like hesitation, deferral, or requests for more support. They look like people asking for your help when what they really need is your belief that they can do it themselves. As a leader, your job is not to take the discomfort away. Your job is to guide people through it. That means holding the line when someone tries to hand you work that belongs to them. It means naming the fear without shaming the person. It means staying calm while someone else flails.

This is where brain-friendly leadership matters. You can use techniques that reduce threat without removing challenge. Ask questions that invite reflection instead of offering answers. Clarify expectations early, so people cannot unconsciously slip away from them. Create moments of stretch, then stay close enough to support, without stepping in to rescue. That is what builds capability. That is what turns dodgers into high-performing team members.

Every project depends on people stepping into responsibility. Ownership is not just about doing tasks. It is about staying with the work emotionally when it gets hard. When you remove that edge, you remove the growth. But when you hold the tension well, something powerful happens. People rise, they surprise themselves, and they start showing up differently, not just for the project, but for everything that follows.

Here's a true story I call: Fear First. Then Confidence. Everything seemed to be going well. I was early in my entrepreneurship journey, and leading people had become a central part of my work. I believed I was doing a good job. People came to me with problems, and I helped them solve them. That felt like leadership.

Then one day, my coach said something that stopped me in my tracks. She told me I was hurting people, not helping them. I could not understand it at first. How could stepping in and offering support be harmful? If someone was overwhelmed, I took the pressure off. I thought that was the right thing to do.

She asked me one question. "Kursten, what do you notice about your team coming to you for help?" At first, I struggled to see it. Then it became clear. I was not building their capability. I was conditioning their dependence. I had taught them that when something felt too uncomfortable, I would take it off their plate.

The day before, a team member had come to me nervous about chairing a meeting. It was her responsibility. She was more than capable, but she felt unsure, and without thinking, I told her I would do it. That moment landed hard. I had stepped in to ease her fear, but in doing so, I had reinforced the idea that discomfort should be avoided.

I went back to her. I explained what I had realized, and we had an honest conversation. She agreed to chair the meeting. She was still nervous, but she was also willing. After a few tries, she told me how proud she felt for stepping up and proving to herself that she could handle it.

That moment changed me. Real growth happens when people choose to move into discomfort, not away from it. Confidence is built through action, not through waiting to feel ready. As leaders, we need to let people stretch. That is how they grow, and that is how we grow too.

Perfectionists: Winning Battles, Losing Wars

Perfectionism is one of the most socially accepted forms of self-sabotage. It hides in plain sight, often rewarded, praised, and mistaken for high standards or professionalism. But beneath the polish is fear. Not just fear of making a mistake, but fear of being exposed, falling short, or appearing inadequate.

Project Pulse

Perfectionism undermines excellence.

It often travels alongside procrastination and overwhelm, but it is not simply a behavior pattern. Perfectionism is a belief system. It tells people that their worth is tied to flawlessness, that safety and belonging come only when everything is done without error. Under that belief, learning becomes dangerous, mistakes become personal, and asking for help begins to feel like failure.

Because perfectionists usually produce well-crafted work, the cost of this mindset is easy to miss. But it is there. It slows down execution. It drains energy. It creates rigid thinking that resists feedback, avoids uncertainty, and struggles to recover from even small missteps. While it may look like discipline or care, perfectionism quietly stifles the very growth it claims to support.

Belief Systems are built one e-mail at a time:

Everything was going well, and the company was growing. I had recently hired a new junior team member who seemed bright, motivated, and eager to contribute. She was stepping into a role with real growth potential, and I was excited to see how she would take it on.

Then a small moment revealed something larger. She needed to send a simple e-mail, nothing complicated, just a short message to move a task forward. But days passed, and the message never went out. When I asked about it, she gave vague answers. She looked busy, but nothing was happening. It was a subtle mix of procrastination and quiet avoidance.

At first, it seemed like she was simply dragging her feet. But when I took a closer look, it became clear the issue was not the e-mail itself. It was what the e-mail represented. She was afraid of getting it wrong, of being judged, of looking unprepared. The task had triggered a deeper fear that had her completely stuck.

I could have stepped in to help, edited the message, or sent it myself to ease the pressure. But that would have taken away her opportunity to grow. Instead, I named what I saw. I told her I believed she could handle it and that learning to sit with discomfort was part of the job.

She resisted at first but followed through. She wrote the e-mail. Then she wrote another. Over time, she stopped second-guessing and began to move forward on her own. Something shifted. Her confidence grew, and she began to take on more responsibility. Eventually, she led a challenging assignment in a new role, not because she suddenly felt ready, but because she had built the capacity to act through discomfort.

That is what real growth looks like. Confidence is not something you wait for. It is something you earn by moving forward, even when part of you wants to hold back.

Helping the Overwhelmed Reclaim Their Power

A person's mental and emotional capacity can be compared to a pipe that carries water. When the pipe is clear, thoughts move in an organized way, energy flows without unnecessary resistance, and the individual can sort through competing priorities with a sense of clarity and control. There is enough internal space to respond with perspective and purpose.

However, when someone is overwhelmed, that pipe becomes clogged. Instead of progressing smoothly, the flow is blocked by self-doubt, unrelenting self-criticism, emotional residue from unresolved experiences, and an ever-present worry about things that cannot be controlled. The system backs up, and even the most routine task begins to feel unmanageable.

This condition is not about personal weakness. It is the result of internal overload. In many cases, the problem is not the size of the workload but the way the person is relating to it. Their attention is consumed by imagined consequences, unrealistic standards, or a persistent fear of disappointing others. As the pressure builds, their cognitive resources become diverted toward internal noise instead of forward motion.

In this moment, the leader's task is not to step in and rearrange the environment or reduce expectations. What the person needs is not relief from responsibility, but a way to reclaim access to their own thinking. That begins by slowing the moment down and helping them notice what is happening. Ask thoughtful questions to uncover the story beneath the overwhelm. What are they assuming about what might happen? What beliefs are influencing their sense of pressure? What internal voice is driving their urgency or despair? Often, just the act of noticing these patterns begins to create relief.

When someone recognizes the thoughts that are clogging their internal pipe, they can begin to let them go. As those thoughts loosen their grip, the sense of pressure eases. Clarity returns. The problem may not have changed, but the person's relationship to it has. With their thinking settled, they are once again able to approach the work with focus, judgment, and creativity.

The job of a leader in these moments is not to provide answers or take tasks away. It is to create space for people to clear out the internal noise that is obstructing their thinking. From that space, movement becomes possible again. And when the pipe is flowing freely, even the most complex challenges begin to feel manageable.

I was consulting on a large transformation, and one part of my role was to support the project lead for a key stream of work. She was young, capable, and bright, but new to leadership and untested in a project of this scale. Early on, I noticed subtle signs of avoidance. Tasks were slipping, decisions dragged, and she quietly redirected responsibilities with comments like, "You're better at this than I am," which appeared collaborative but revealed deeper hesitation.

As a major milestone approached, a key team member left the project. The pressure that had been building quietly began to show. Her confidence began to erode. She withdrew, avoided key conversations, and her energy faded. In our coaching sessions, it became clear that her thinking had been overtaken by self-doubt. She was plagued by thoughts like, "What if I fail?" and "Someone like me should not be leading something this important." The temporary nature of her role only amplified her fear, making every decision feel like a test of her worth.

That fear consumed her mental capacity. Her days were filled, but little progress was made. It was not a lack of skill that was holding her back. It was the noise of worry, self-judgment, and fear of being exposed. Rather than stepping in with advice or solutions, I asked questions to help her examine the beliefs beneath her stress. As she began to untangle those thoughts, her posture changed. Her voice steadied. The fog began to lift.

In the weeks that followed, she started showing up differently. She took ownership, made timely decisions, and faced problems head-on. Her thinking had cleared, and her leadership followed. Within a few months, she was offered a permanent role in another part of the organization, a recognition of the potential she had unlocked.

Her progress came not from knowing all the answers but from reclaiming the mental space that fear had filled. Once that cleared, her ability to lead came through fully.

What to do When Everything Seems Stuck

Projects are ultimately human systems. That means they succeed or fail based not just on tasks and timelines, but on how people think, feel, and respond under pressure. To lead effectively in that environment, you need to understand what drives human behavior. And the driving force is emotion, not logic. In particular, fear shows up constantly in project work, usually unspoken and often disguised.

The SCARF model (Status, Certainty, Autonomy, Relatedness, and Fairness), developed by David Rock, gives us a way to understand how people experience social threat and reward. These five domains shape how people interpret the world around them. When one of these elements feels under threat, the nervous system treats it as if the threat were physical. The brain shifts into survival mode. Fight, flight, or freeze responses kick in. Rational thinking fades. Creativity and collaboration shut down. What remains is a narrowed focus on self-preservation.

This explains so much of what we see in project teams. Avoidance, defensiveness, micromanagement, silence in meetings, endless overpreparation, refusal to commit, or even sabotage. These are not character flaws. They are fear responses.

Part of your job as a project leader is to guide the rhythm of the team. That means helping people shift between different parts of their brain. When the reptilian brain is in charge, behavior becomes rigid and reactive. To access the prefrontal cortex, where creativity, planning, and critical thinking live, people need to feel safe enough to loosen their grip on control. That safety does not mean comfort. It means finding the right balance between challenge and support.

SCARF gives you a way to map the terrain. It helps you understand what might be triggering fear in a particular person. Is it uncertainty about what success looks like? Is it a loss of autonomy in decision making? Is it a perceived unfairness in how work is being assigned? Once you build a model for what might be threatening for each team member, you can begin tailoring how you communicate, how you give feedback, and how you interpret resistance or conflict when it arises.

The goal is not to remove all threats. That is impossible and, frankly, not desirable. The goal is to find the edge of growth. Too little threat and nothing changes. Too much and people shut down. The sweet spot is stretch. It is the place where people lean into their discomfort, take steps forward, and build capacity through challenge. As a leader, you are constantly tuning that edge.

When you understand how people experience threat and reward, you stop reacting to surface behavior and start addressing what is actually driving it. That is where real leadership begins.

Once you start looking through this lens, patterns begin to emerge. What often gets dismissed as laziness, poor communication, or lack of discipline is usually something deeper. These behaviors are signals.

They are how fear speaks when it has no language of its own and once you know what to look for, you see them everywhere. In the next sections, I will walk through some of the most common fear-based behaviors that show up in project teams. These are the silent killers of progress; they drain momentum, erode trust, and stall delivery, and they are far more common than most leaders are willing to admit.

When a project grinds to a halt, it can be tempting to draw quick conclusions. It may seem like someone is holding things up, avoiding responsibility, or quietly resisting the work. The human mind naturally fills in the blanks with a narrative, trying to make sense of the slowdown by assigning motives and explanations. But the danger with this pattern is that once a story takes hold, it becomes difficult to see beyond it. It closes off curiosity, locks in assumptions, and limits your ability to understand what is truly happening underneath the surface.

Rather than acting out the story your brain has created, a far more effective approach is to build a working model of the person's perspective. This means observing their behavior without judgment, asking questions that surface their beliefs, and considering what might be shaping their reactions. People rarely behave irrationally for no reason. Most of the time, they are doing the best they can based on the thinking they have access to and the constraints they believe they are operating within. Your task as a leader is to slow down your interpretations long enough to see the internal logic behind their choices, even if those choices are not serving the project.

Narrative is one of the most powerful diagnostic tools a leader can use to understand how someone is experiencing their work. The way people describe situations, assign meaning, and choose their language reveals how they are interpreting the world around them. These are not just casual comments or throwaway phrases. They are clues. A comment about how a decision was made without consultation might really be saying, "I do not feel heard." A complaint about timelines being unrealistic could be masking a belief that they are being set up to fail. Even silence in meetings, when someone has something valuable to contribute but says nothing, may be their way of expressing, "It does not feel safe to speak." These moments are not just functional communication. They are emotional signals, and those signals tell you where someone may be stuck, where fear has crept in, and where their sense of agency is beginning to collapse.

Listening carefully to the narrative someone uses allows you to spot patterns in thinking that may be holding them back. Stories that center on blame, helplessness, or avoidance are often signs that the person feels overwhelmed or disconnected from a sense of agency. Sometimes those narratives come from past experiences where speaking up did not help or taking initiative led to criticism. Other times, they are the result of chronic stress or a culture that subtly rewards compliance over ownership. Whatever the source, those patterns become habits. Left unexamined, they shape how people approach problems, make decisions, and engage with others.

The good news is that these narratives are not fixed. They can be explored, tested, and rewritten. To do that, you have to stay curious. You cannot afford to take what someone says at face value and assume it reflects the full truth. You need to ask better questions. What leads you to think that? What would happen if you tried something different? These questions invite people to reflect rather than defend. They create space for new insights to emerge and for stuck thinking to loosen its grip. Over time, this is how new stories begin to take root as stories grounded not in fear or resignation, but in agency, capability, and possibility.

In financial markets, the VIX, also known as the volatility index, acts as a real-time measure of investor anxiety. When uncertainty rises, the index spikes, signaling that fear is shaping decision making across the market. When confidence returns, the index falls, suggesting that people are thinking clearly again. While projects do not have a formal VIX, they absolutely have a similar emotional rhythm. I refer to this as the Project VIX, and once you learn to notice it, you can begin to sense when a project is tipping from clarity into chaos.

Projects generate emotional volatility because they introduce uncertainty, visibility, accountability, and change. These conditions stir anxiety, and when that anxiety builds unaddressed, it begins to hijack how people think, speak, and act. The Project VIX rises when tension enters the room, when meetings feel charged or reactive, or when people start guarding information, shifting blame, or avoiding decisions. It is not always loud. Sometimes it shows up as silence. Sometimes as sarcasm, passive resistance, or unnecessary complexity that hides indecision.

When the emotional volatility in a project rises, people do not make better choices by pushing harder or speeding up. Instead, the nervous system is already flooded. What is needed is a pause to lower the threat level. People need help to see clearly again, to regulate their responses, and to return to thoughtful decision making. When you can sense the Project VIX rising, your job as a leader is to bring that fear back down so the team can recover its rhythm and focus.

Most people believe they make decisions based on logic. They tell themselves they are rational, that their choices are guided by careful thought and analysis. But in reality, emotion almost always gets there first. The moment before a decision is made, especially in high-pressure environments like projects, is often shaped by fear, not logic. That moment is what I call the longest second.

Picture this. A senior leader asks one of your team members to take on a new responsibility, something they have never done before. The request seems simple enough. Facilitate a meeting, lead a workstream, deliver a tough message. But as soon as the words land, something happens inside them. A sensation in the pit of their stomach, a tightening in their chest, or a flutter of anxiety they cannot quite name. That physical reaction is the nervous system interpreting the request as a threat. It happens instantly, long before their logical mind catches up.

In that split second, they begin to look for a way out. Not because they are unwilling or incompetent, but because they are uncomfortable. And instead of naming the discomfort, they begin to rationalize their way around it. I am already too busy. It would be better if someone else did it. I do not want to risk the optics. I need to protect my work–life balance. These are not lies. They are emotional cover stories that help the person avoid what they fear without having to confront it directly.

If you are not paying attention, these moments pass by unnoticed. The person ducks the assignment, someone else steps in, and life moves on. But something important just happened. A growth opportunity was lost. The person missed a chance to confront the fear, regulate through it, and emerge stronger on the other side.

As a leader, your job is not to push people into situations they are not ready for. But it is also not your job to protect them from every discomfort. You need to recognize when someone is having a longest second moment, and help them stay with it just long enough to see it clearly. That means slowing things down, naming the tension, and asking questions that open up their thinking. What is it about this ask that feels uncomfortable? What story are you telling yourself about what might happen? What would it look like to try, even if it is not perfect?

These are the moments that shape people. Not the big speeches or dramatic turning points, but the quiet seconds where someone chooses to lean in instead of stepping away. When leaders learn to work with those moments instead of rushing past them, everything changes. Confidence is built. Capacity grows. And over time, the team becomes stronger than it was before.

Sometimes, despite your best efforts, the outcome is clear. You have provided support. You have offered coaching and have been patient and clear. And still, the person has not shifted. This does not make them bad or broken. It simply means there is a misalignment between what the role requires and how they are currently thinking and behaving. When someone remains stuck in patterns of avoidance, resistance, or fear, even after support, it is time to move from development to decision. You can't want it more than they do.

At this point, the responsibility solely rests with them. You must be clear about what is expected and where they are falling short. You cannot force growth; you can only create the conditions and hold the standard. If they are unwilling or unable to meet it, then you must act. That may mean letting them go. It may mean helping them find a different role that is a better fit for how they operate. Either way, clarity protects both the team and the individual.

This is not about control or blame. It is about creating alignment. It is about ensuring that the people on your team are capable of doing the work and growing with the demands of the role. When someone is not a fit, the most respectful and responsible thing you can do is name it and take action. At the end of the day, you're actually helping them by allowing them to find something that's better aligned with their abilities.

CHAPTER 10

Growth Is Your Greatest Competitive Advantage

Many people equate growth with gaining knowledge. They imagine that growth means acquiring more information, mastering more technical tools, or accumulating credentials. But what if the real transformation is not in what you know, but in how you think? What if I told you that growth is about reshaping the foundation of your thinking itself?

To grow is to ascend. It is to move through the pyramid rather than getting stuck at its base. It is to stop collecting answers and begin building the thinking that allows you to ask the right questions, interpret the right signals, and decide what matters most. Growth is not about knowing more. Growth is about becoming wise.

Your Personal Solar System: Curate it Carefully

There are a few things in life that we can truly control, but one of them is profoundly powerful. We have the ability to decide who we allow into our lives and how much influence they have over us. This decision, often overlooked or taken for granted, sets the trajectory of everything else.

Think of your life as a solar system. You are the sun at the center. The people in your life become planets, moons, and asteroids. However, unlike our solar system, you choose who gets to enter your solar system, how closely you allow them to orbit, and just as importantly, who gets to stay. You have the power to allow people into your gravitational field and the authority to eject them when necessary. The cumulative effect of who is in your orbit and how much gravity you permit them to exert determines the long-term direction of your life.

You are not a passive participant in this system. You are its designer. That means your responsibility is to construct a solar system that reflects where you want to go, not where you have been. This is not about being selective in an elitist sense. It is about being intentional in a strategic sense. If you surround yourself with people who want to see you succeed, who believe in your potential, and who have the skills to support you in positive, constructive ways, then growth becomes inevitable. These individuals help you expand, not by pushing you directly, but by elevating the environment around you through access to their thinking.

On the other hand, if your orbit is crowded with people who are self-serving, who extract more than they contribute, or who manipulate your energy to serve their own needs, then your progress will remain slow and uncertain. It is not enough to want growth. You have to protect the conditions that allow it to take root.

In my own life, I have benefited immensely from individuals who have shaped my thinking and challenged me to grow. One of them is a coach whose mental maps are entirely different from my own. By spending time with him regularly, reading his content, and attending his growth experiences, I find that his way of thinking begins to influence mine. It happens slowly, often in ways that are invisible on the surface, but over time those small shifts compound into meaningful change.

Another has been a long-time mentor who held senior roles as a chief executive officer and other similar positions. Over the years, he has not only mentored me but also opened doors to opportunities that aligned with my strengths while still stretching my abilities. Now retired, he continues to meet with me regularly. Our conversations span a wide range of topics, and each one gives me the chance to sharpen my critical thinking and refine my mental models.

Designing your solar system is not a one-time decision. It is a continuous and deliberate act, one that requires reflection, courage, and a deep commitment to your own growth.

Discipline: The Bridge Between Goals and Results

It is easy to begin something when motivation is high, and the possibilities feel wide open. It is far more difficult to persist when the results are not yet visible, and the early momentum has faded. Yet this is the very essence of growth. You cannot accomplish anything meaningful unless you are willing to sustain disciplined effort long before any visible payoff appears. *Immediate gratification often creates immediate failure.*

Growth demands this discipline more than almost any other pursuit. It is not a short burst of energy. It is not a checklist you complete and move on from. It is a lifelong commitment. If you choose to keep growing, then you are also choosing to keep showing up. Often, that means returning to the same practices for months or even years, long before any evidence tells you that the work is paying off.

Along the way, you will face moments that challenge everything. You may experience setbacks so intense that they feel like personal losses. You might lose a business. You might remove a partner or a close friend from your closest orbits. The path to growth is often marked by decisions that others do not understand and sacrifices that feel overwhelming in the moment.

This is why discipline matters. Our minds are constantly working to keep us safe, but that same instinct can become a prison. The brain tends to fixate on the most catastrophic version of the future, then uses that imagined disaster to justify inaction. *When you tell yourself you cannot afford to fail, what you are really doing is making it impossible to succeed.* The only way forward is to act anyway, to show up long before results emerge, and to give yourself the chance to reach what you cannot yet see.

In my own journey, I reached a turning point when I left a well-paying corporate job that I had spent over a decade building. I was not stagnating, but I was no longer growing at the pace I knew I needed. Something in me was moving faster than the environment around me. I needed space to match my velocity. On the day I resigned, my senior vice president happened to be in town. I went to tell him in person. His response was immediate. He looked at me and said, "You are making the biggest mistake of your life."

Despite the gravity of that moment, I continued forward. I could not articulate it fully at the time, but what I was really doing was rearranging my solar system. I was creating the conditions that would allow me to grow on my own terms. The early stages were not easy. There were bumps, setbacks, and long stretches of uncertainty. But that discipline, the decision to keep showing up every day, became the foundation for everything that followed. After a few months, I was having dinner and a glass of wine with the same senior vice president at his favorite Italian restaurant, and he admitted, "I can see why you made the decision to leave." He continued to mentor me despite our being competitors until his unexpected passing.

Over time, I shifted from running projects to providing advisory services. The value I offered began to stem not from how much time I put in, but from the clarity and depth of my thinking. That shift unlocked new income streams and gave me the ability to build a more balanced life. It also led to breakthroughs in areas I never expected. One of the most surprising was in investing. The same mental discipline I had cultivated through years of growth allowed me to make more thoughtful, more emotionally regulated investment decisions.

There is a hidden truth about growth that most people never talk about. When you have the discipline to show up, the effort often feels disconnected. You learn something new here. You practice a new behavior there. None of it seems to produce much change. But if you stay with it long enough, something powerful happens. You reach a "gel point."

The gel point is the moment when all the individual elements you have been working on quietly come together. It is often subtle. It does not announce itself in advance. But in that moment, your thinking, your skills, and your mindset click into alignment. What was once scattered and abstract becomes clear and usable. The progress becomes real.

Project Pulse

The Gel Point, when everything you've been practicing clicks in one harmonious event.

For me, one of the clearest gel points came in the way I interact with people. Early in my career, I was not a great listener. I thought I was, but I was often more focused on what I wanted to say next than on what the other person was actually communicating. I began to work on this. I practiced paraphrasing. I asked better questions. I mirrored. I stayed quiet longer. I paid attention to emotion as well as logic. For a long time, it felt like slow progress. But then, over time, it gelled.

Suddenly, I could feel the shift in real conversations. I was no longer trying to remember which tool to use. I was dancing with the moment, fully present, responding with clarity and precision, and that changed everything. I began to influence conversations in ways that created real movement. I could guide stakeholders in the direction that a project or a team needed to go, not through pressure, but through resonance. That is the power of the gel point, and it only comes if you have the discipline to keep showing up, long before you know when the moment will arrive.

Practice: The Path to Mastery

Discipline is what gets you moving toward great success. Practice is what transforms you once you are there.

Many people confuse discipline and practice. They imagine that showing up day after day is enough. But discipline is only the precondition. It is the habit of returning. Practice, by contrast, is what you *do* with that time. It is the deliberate, focused effort to refine your skill, stretch your awareness, and deepen your understanding. It is the difference between going through the motions and engaging in purposeful repetition that leads to change.

Mastery does not emerge from routine alone. It comes from the kind of practice that is intentional, feedback-rich, and grounded in reflection. True practice is not passive. It does not merely involve putting in the hours. It demands presence. It demands curiosity. It demands the humility to examine what is not yet working and the courage to keep adjusting until it does.

This is where experimentation plays a critical role. You have to be willing to design small, deliberate experiments that stretch your current capacity. Growth does not happen by accident. It happens when you choose to try something different. You might decide, for example, that you will practice asking at least one "what or how" question in your next conversation, instead of asking a "yes or no" one. That one decision becomes the experiment. You observe how it feels. You notice the response. You reflect on what worked and what did not. These small trials build insight. They reveal the gap between intention and execution, and they invite you to keep refining. If it feels clumsy, then you know you're in the right place.

In this sense, practice is not about perfection. It is about progression. It is about turning attention into improvement. Over time, what begins as awkward becomes fluid. What once felt foreign becomes second nature. But this transformation is not linear. Progress often comes in waves, and the most meaningful gains are rarely immediate. What you are really building is a new mental model, a new way of seeing and responding that ultimately becomes part of who you are.

One of the clearest examples of what true practice looks like came from watching our daughter learn to speak. At first, she made sounds that seemed chaotic. There were gurgles, growls, and bursts of breath and saliva. But they were not chaotic at all. She was experimenting. She was trying different positions of her tongue, exploring how her mouth moved, and playing with the force and rhythm of her breath. Each sound was a small test. She was mapping the territory of possibility. She had no fear of getting it wrong. She did not pause to judge whether the sound made sense or whether it came out clearly. She simply practiced, again and again, guided by instinct and curiosity.

She was not learning the way most adults attempt to learn, by gathering knowledge first and then trying to apply it later. She was learning by doing, by adjusting in real time, by listening to us and slowly closing the gap between the sounds we made and the ones she could produce. This was practice in its purest form, full of experimentation and free from fear. And then one day it happened. She spoke her first word, and it was unmistakable. The syllables came together with clarity and purpose. That was her gel point. All the scattered effort, all the small, repeated trials, all the invisible groundwork suddenly came together. The sounds were no longer disconnected. The practice had taken root, and something new had emerged.

You can apply this idea of practice to any domain. You might practice giving feedback. You might practice strategic thinking. You might practice staying calm under pressure. No matter the area, the principle remains: The quality of your practice determines the speed and depth of your growth. Practice creates compound interest in your abilities. The longer you engage with it, the more transformative the returns become.

When I began coaching, one of the hardest things to develop was the ability to listen and ask meaningful questions. It did not come naturally. For most of my life, I had been taught to offer answers, to solve problems, and to give people something they could take away and act on. That impulse to fix and direct was deeply ingrained. In the early stages, even remembering to pause and ask a question required conscious effort. The flow of conversation felt interrupted, and the questions I asked landed awkwardly. They lacked depth and intention. Many were closed in form, designed to produce a quick yes or no rather than open a space for reflection.

Instead of pulling back, I leaned in. I treated the process as a series of experiments. I tried asking different kinds of questions, focusing more on what and how rather than why. I began to notice how the structure of a question could shift the energy in the room. I allowed silence to stretch longer than felt comfortable, watching what might emerge within it. I paid attention not only to what people said, but to how they said it, observing their tone, their pace, and their posture. I practiced consistently, not to perform a skill, but to understand something deeper. I wanted to learn how to guide someone toward their own insight without trying to carry them there myself.

Over time, something began to change. I no longer needed to remind myself to ask a question or second-guess whether it was the right one. My presence in conversation became more grounded. The questions came more freely. They carried less judgment and more curiosity. I could feel when a question landed well, when it created movement inside the other person, and when it gave them access to something they had not seen before. The people I worked with began to shift, not because I was giving better advice, but because I had learned to stay in the conversation without rushing toward solutions. That change did not come from talent. It came from the willingness to experiment. It came from the choice to keep practicing when the results were not immediate. And it came from trusting that if I stayed with the process, it would eventually lead to something more powerful than I could have planned.

Ultimately, mastery is not a destination. *It is a relationship with practice.* It is the quiet decision to stay in the work, to remain teachable, and to move toward excellence even when no one is watching. The path to mastery is paved not with talent, but with sustained, intentional practice. And to achieve that, you need to keep a positive perspective on life.

Positive Psychology: Your Unfair Advantage

If you want to keep practicing, you need a reason to return. That reason is rarely found in data or discipline alone. It comes from your internal narrative, the story you tell yourself about who you are, what you are doing, and why it matters. That story is not fixed. It can ebb and flow. Some days, it will be quiet and steady. Other days, it may feel fragile or uncertain. But underneath those variations, you need a current of belief that what you are doing has purpose. Without that belief, it becomes difficult to show up at all.

This is where the principles of positive psychology come in. A positive mindset is not about pretending that everything is fine. It is not about forced optimism. It is about cultivating a deeper sense of agency, meaning, and possibility. When you believe that growth is possible, when you see setbacks as temporary, and when you trust that your effort contributes to something worthwhile, you are far more likely to return to the work. You are far more likely to keep showing up and practicing, even when the results are not immediate.

Action is what gets you started. It is the first move. Discipline is what keeps that movement alive over time. It is the structure that supports consistency. But practice is what transforms your effort into learning. Practice is what turns raw action into something deliberate, something that builds skill, insight, and growth. For all of that to work, your mindset matters. If your internal narrative is rooted in discouragement, you will hesitate to begin. If it is clouded by doubt, you will struggle to persist. But when your story carries even a modest sense of hope or direction, you create the conditions for meaningful, lasting progress.

You do not need to feel great every day. *But if you want to build something meaningful over time, then the story you carry inside you matters.* You need to believe there is value in showing up. You need to believe that growth is possible. Without that, even the best tools and practices will eventually fall away. With it, you create the conditions for sustained effort, deeper learning, and transformation that lasts.

Optimism is not a fixed trait. It is a skill that can be learned. This is one of the most important findings from Seligman's work discussed in his book *Learned Optimism*.[1] It is easy to assume that some people are naturally more hopeful or more resilient, but the truth is far more encouraging. Optimism is not about ignoring difficulty or pretending that everything will turn out well. It is about learning to interpret setbacks in ways that keep you engaged. When you train yourself to view adversity as temporary rather than permanent, as specific rather than universal, and as influenced by external factors rather than as a personal failure, you create space to continue. This shift in interpretation can be practiced. It is a form of mental training that strengthens your ability to persevere. It creates the conditions that make discipline possible and practice meaningful. Without that shift, your internal story can quietly persuade you that effort is wasted. With it, you are much more likely to return to the work and keep moving forward, even when progress is hard to see.

The ability to reinterpret setbacks is not only a psychological advantage. It is a foundation for something deeper. *Optimism creates the conditions for persistence, but resiliency is what allows you to stand back up when things fall apart.* If optimism is the belief that forward movement is possible, resiliency is the strength to keep moving when the path becomes steep, uncertain, or painful. Together, they form the emotional core of sustained growth. Without that core, even the most disciplined effort will eventually begin to crack. It is not enough to practice when things are going well. You also need the capacity to return when everything feels difficult, confusing, or unfair. The result is resiliency.

Resiliency: Your Unshakable Foundation

Resiliency is not the same as toughness. It is not about suppressing emotion or pretending nothing affects you. It is closer to the strength of a well-designed material, one that can bear weight while still allowing for movement. A rigid structure may appear solid, but it cracks under strain. A soft one may bend too easily and fail to offer support. The most resilient

---

[1] Vintage, 2006.

systems are those that can absorb impact, adjust to new forces, and return to their shape without losing integrity. The same is true for people.

Some materials appear strong but fail under stress. Glass can carry weight and hold its shape with precision, but the moment pressure arrives from an unexpected angle, it shatters. Ceramic has similar limits. It looks solid, feels strong, yet it cracks without warning. On the other end of the spectrum, soft materials like foam or rubber deform easily. They stretch and absorb force, but they collapse when asked to bear real weight. They give way without offering support. True resilience lives somewhere between these two extremes. It is the strength of tempered steel, which can hold a load without fracturing, and still flex under strain. It is the intelligence of bamboo, which bends in the wind and returns upright. Resilient materials are not weak. They are not brittle. They are designed to respond. They absorb pressure, adapt to change, and return to form without losing their strength. Resilient people do the same.

Resiliency is not built on force. It is built on recovery. You do not need to push through everything with intensity and pressure. What you need is the capacity to feel what is difficult without being undone by it. You need the honesty to name what has been lost or shaken, the clarity to see what is still present, and the strength to return to the work with steadiness. Resilience is the result of emotional skill. It allows you to come back, not dulled or detached, but more present, more aware, and more prepared.

That return is not about restoring what was. It is not about coming back to the same place. Alan Weiss says that true resilience is not about bouncing back. *It is about bouncing forward.* You do not return unchanged. If you choose, you come back wiser and carry a new perspective with deeper instincts and a refined understanding of what matters. The difficulty becomes part of your evolution, not a detour from it.

This is also where resilience connects directly to identity. Each time you face something hard and stay with it, you are not just managing difficulty. You are building your own belief, and you are strengthening your sense of self. Confidence does not come before you move; it comes after. That confidence does not come from praise or comfort. It comes from evidence. It comes from having done something hard and knowing you are still standing. Psychologists call this self-efficacy. It is the belief that you can influence outcomes, that your actions have weight. It is one of the most powerful predictors of future performance. And it is cultivated, not inherited.

Resilience is not a trait; it's the result of practice and growth. It becomes part of you through repetition, reflection, and experience. You earn it not because life gets easier, but because you stop avoiding what is hard. You meet it with presence, move through it with strength, and you come out the other side with more of yourself intact.

Let's now turn to a "healthy selfishness" that will allow you to continue to grow while contributing mightily to others.

CHAPTER 11

Play Your Own Game,
Not Theirs

External pressures mislead us about what investing our time into is actually high value and what is superfluous. Energy is spent on things beyond our control. The ability to prioritize and let go of low-value investments in the face of normative pressure allows us to get to the destination we are striving for. We reap the harvest only after investing in undertakings in spring and nurturing them through the summer to give the potential for a bountiful harvest in fall.

There comes a point in every career when something shifts. For some, it arrives in a quiet moment. For others, it feels more like a jolt. Either way, the realization is the same. You have been following someone else's script. You have invested your energy trying to meet expectations that were never truly yours. You have made decisions for approval instead of alignment. Outwardly, everything may seem fine, although beneath the surface, a quiet unease begins to grow. That unease is not a failure; it is a signal. It is the first sign that you are ready to make a change, *because you need to create your own metrics, not appropriate someone else's.*

This chapter is about reclaiming authorship of your story. We begin by redefining value, not in the eyes of others, but in terms of what creates lasting and meaningful impact in life and business. We examine how to focus your energy where it counts, rather than wasting it on distraction or image. We look at prioritization not as a productivity strategy, but as a gateway to breathing room and clear choices. We return to your true direction, the deeper current that keeps you steady. And we close with a reminder from the seasons of the farm. The work that matters most often begins quietly, with a single seed planted in the soil, far from anyone's attention, but full of possibility.

Redefining "High Value" on Your Own Terms

Most people never take the time to define what "high value" means for them. Instead, they inherit someone else's version of it. They absorb expectations from clients, managers, peers, and even vague professional norms without ever questioning whether those expectations are useful or even accurate. The result is a kind of "unconscious outsourcing" of values. People learn to perform the role of the high-achiever while forgetting to examine whether their actions actually make anything better. A consultant becomes known for being agreeable, flexible, and responsive. Clients enjoy working with them, but over time, the value of the work begins to fade. Their insights are safe, their recommendations obvious, and their efforts aligned more with perception than with meaningful outcomes. Without realizing it, they have traded value for approval.

This raises a fundamental question: whose scorecard are you playing with? Too often, we find ourselves measuring our success using someone else's metrics. We aim to appear indispensable instead of being effective. We respond quickly to e-mails because it makes us look responsive, not because it helps move the work forward. We fill our calendars with meetings, not because they are essential, but because they are visible. We craft updates and decks for stakeholders who will never read them. This is performance, not value. The moment we internalize someone else's scoreboard, we begin chasing visibility instead of impact. And the deeper that pattern sets in, the harder it becomes to step back and notice that we are no longer playing our own game.

There is a difference that separates people who stay busy from those who make things better. That difference is the gap between effort and effect. Effort consumes time, attention, and energy. It satisfies expectations. It fills calendars and creates a sense of motion. It is immediate gratification. Often, it feels like progress. It carries the appearance of dedication and professionalism.

Yet it does not always lead to improvement. Activity on its own does not produce outcomes. Effect, by contrast, is what actually changes the situation. It is the tangible result. It is the movement of a problem toward resolution. It is the creation of something useful, lasting, or clear. Effect is not to be confused with affect, which in psychology refers to emotion or its expression.

Effort tends to show up in familiar patterns. It is present when you join a meeting because your presence signals involvement, even if your contribution is unnecessary. It appears when you answer e-mails within minutes, not because they are important, but because responsiveness makes you seem committed. It emerges in the hours spent refining presentations, reports, and updates that few will ever read. These documents become symbolic proof of effort rather than tools for decision making or insight. Effort also reveals itself when you agree to a client request that reduces short-term anxiety while leaving the real problem untouched. You may find yourself allowing urgency to dictate your actions even when your experience tells you the urgency is misplaced.

The effect calls for a different posture. It begins with the willingness to step away from surface-level activity and focus on what actually needs to change. That might mean declining a meeting in order to create uninterrupted time for real problem-solving. It might involve offering a client an uncomfortable truth rather than a polished response designed to reassure. It could mean building a process no one requested because you saw the opportunity to make something better. It may include writing or creating something that will not gain attention now, but will carry weight later for the people who need it. In some cases, it will mean choosing rest, not as a form of escape, but as a way to return to the work with renewed clarity, fresh perspective, and the energy to lead.

The professional world tends to reward visible effort because it is easier to notice and simpler to measure. (We always thank the people who arrive in the office early to make coffee for everyone, and tend to overlook the fact that their contributions to work are often late.) Tasks and timelines provide structure. Activity becomes the default indicator of commitment. Responses delivered with speed are often mistaken for results. However, the contributions that leave the deepest mark rarely emerge from motion alone. They come from individuals who slow down enough to think clearly, act with purpose, and remain loyal to outcomes rather than appearances. Choosing effect over effort is not an argument against hard work. It is an argument for meaningful work.

Creating value requires looking beyond what is immediately in front of you. It involves resisting the pull of short-term convenience in order to act in the service of long-term outcomes. In many situations, what feels easier in the moment leads to consequences that gradually reshape the culture, the work, or the path forward. Although these effects may not be visible right away, they often carry more weight than the original decision. Leaders who create value learn to think beyond the immediate. They consider what their actions will set in motion. They make decisions that account for the second- and third-order effects, recognizing that lasting results come from what is sustained, not what is hurried.

One common example emerges inside project teams. Imagine you are working with people who have developed a pattern of avoiding responsibility. Over time, they begin to miss key commitments, distance themselves from ownership, and quietly allow tasks to fall through without accountability. You recognize what is happening, yet you choose not to address it. Perhaps you want to preserve harmony. Perhaps the timing feels inconvenient. Perhaps you hope the behavior will correct itself. In that moment, remaining silent feels easier than creating tension. The short-term return is the avoidance of discomfort.

However, your silence sends a message. The second-order effect is that this behavior becomes normalized. The team member senses that no clear expectation exists. As a result, the pattern continues unchecked. Once reinforced, it begins to shape the tone and expectations of the group. That influence becomes more visible through a third-order effect. Other team members notice the lack of accountability and start to question what matters. Some disengage quietly. Others lower their own standards. Over time, the culture begins to drift. The loss of trust and shared ownership does not happen all at once. It begins with small moments that seem inconsequential yet eventually weaken the integrity of the whole.

Both consequences *and lack of consequences* can create norms.

A similar pattern plays out in more personal decisions. Suppose you have a vision to write a book. You believe in the value of the idea and understand that it could become a meaningful contribution. Still, the writing continues to slide down the list of priorities. It quietly competes with more immediate demands. Billable work comes first. Client expectations press in. Family obligations and routine tasks begin to fill the day. The book is not urgent, so it remains unfinished. The return feels uncertain, and so the work feels optional. Yet when you choose to begin anyway, you create the possibility of a different trajectory. The second-order effect might be the sense of enjoyment and creative alignment that emerges in the process. You may experience sharper thinking, greater confidence in your voice, and a clearer articulation of your ideas. As the work takes shape, third-order effects begin to unfold. The book may build your reputation. It may help others see your perspective more clearly. It may lead to invitations, clients, or opportunities that would never have surfaced had you kept waiting for the right time.

Creating value begins by thinking beyond today. It requires the discipline to pause and ask what a decision is likely to produce over time. It asks you to recognize not only what you are choosing, but what you are making possible by choosing it. These moments are rarely loud. Often, they are buried beneath distraction, urgency, and the pressure to stay busy. Filtering out that noise is part of the discipline. Progress becomes possible when you place your energy into decisions that offer a high return across time. Those are the decisions that change your direction. Those are the ones that change your life.

Channel Energy Into Your Circle of Control

One of the most valuable skills leaders can develop is the ability to distinguish between what is truly within their control, what they can only influence, and what lies entirely outside their reach. The more clearly you can draw those boundaries, the more effectively you can direct your time, energy, and attention to where it will actually make a difference. When you try to hold on to things that you cannot possibly manage, the result is often exhaustion, frustration, and an ongoing sense of overwhelm.

The human brain is wired to react strongly when it perceives a threat, whether that threat is physical or psychological. In a work environment, that reaction might be triggered by uncertainty, by shifting priorities, or by someone else's decision that affects you. The trouble is that our nervous system does not distinguish much between what we can change and what we cannot. We can find ourselves burning energy trying to push against immovable walls, draining the very focus we need for the actions that are actually possible.

I grew up on a grain farm in Canada, where the growing season was short and the climate unforgiving. It was dry-land farming, which meant no irrigation, and the window between frosts was narrow. Every year, frost lingered well into May and returned again in September. In fact, I saw frost or even snow in every month of the year except July. The land was classified as semi-arid desert, and rainfall was always in short supply.

There was only so much you could influence in that environment. You could decide how to prepare the land, choose which crops to plant and the genetics that would give them the best chance, apply herbicide to control weeds, and make sure the machinery was ready for the work ahead. Beyond that, it was out of your hands. You had no control over the amount of rain or sun, the arrival of insects, or the spread of disease.

One year, we seemed to have everything working in our favor. It was shaping up to be one of the best seasons I could remember. The stand-out was a wheat crop we had planted right at the beginning of June, far later than usual. Despite the late start, it was thriving and promised a phenomenal yield. Then, in August, an early frost hit while the wheat was flowering, wiping out seed production entirely. All that potential was gone in a single cold night.

The loss cut deeper because you could not simply walk away. Even though that crop was destroyed, the land still had to be prepared for the next season. That meant more time, more fuel, and more money going out, all with little coming in on those acres. Farming taught me that lesson early: you can only control so much, and once you have done your part, the rest is up to forces beyond you. The sooner you let go of what you cannot change, the sooner you can focus on what comes next.

Ruthless Prioritization: The Key to Breathing Room

One of the hardest disciplines for any leader is saying "no." We hesitate because we do not want to disappoint, we fear missing opportunities, or we worry about how it might be perceived. Every "no" we deliver carries with it an invisible "yes." Saying no to a new initiative may be saying yes to completing the work that truly matters. Declining another meeting may be saying yes to uninterrupted time for thinking, planning, or connecting with the team.

Prioritization is not simply about arranging a list of tasks. It is about deciding what will not be done at all. Strategic neglect is the recognition that you cannot do everything and still maintain clarity and quality. The Pareto principle, often called the 80/20 rule, shows that a relatively small percentage of activities generate most of the results. When you apply this principle, you begin to see that the majority of your impact comes from a small set of focused actions. The rest, no matter how appealing or urgent it might seem, often distracts from core objectives.

Leaders who embrace ruthless prioritization understand that time and energy are finite. They channel attention toward the initiatives that will create the greatest value and deliberately release the rest. This is not carelessness or avoidance. It is the discipline of making hard choices that creates space for the work that actually moves the needle. Without that discipline, you risk filling your days with the noise of endless activity while starving the few efforts that could make a real difference.

Stay Aimed at Your North Star

Purpose is one of the most powerful forces that sustain us through challenges and setbacks. Martin Seligman's work in positive psychology has shown that purpose is a key ingredient in resilience and well-being. It gives meaning to effort and keeps you moving forward even when conditions are difficult. Without purpose, the demands of leadership can feel endless and draining. With purpose, those same demands become part of a larger journey that you believe in.

Your North Star will not always appear in perfect clarity. It is natural for purpose to emerge gradually as you gain experience and perspective. In the early stages, you may be navigating instinctively toward something that feels important without having a complete picture of what it is. This is like steering toward magnetic north rather than true north. The course may not be perfectly straight, but as you gain new insights, you can reorient and bring your direction into sharper focus. Trust that this process is part of the work and that clarity often grows out of movement.

A clear sense of purpose does not mean rigidly holding to a fixed plan. The environment will change, priorities will shift, and new opportunities will appear. Adaptability allows you to stay committed to your North Star while adjusting your path to meet the realities in front of you. Leaders who can adapt without losing sight of their ultimate direction create momentum in all conditions. They bend without breaking, adjust without losing commitment, and remain steady in vision while flexible in execution.

Seasons on the Farm: Plant Some Seeds

Life on the farm moves to a rhythm that does not rush for anyone, and in Canada, that rhythm is shaped by winters that are not merely quiet but unyielding in their severity. January and February bring a depth of cold that could make an engine seize just by looking at it, with days so short the sun seems to rise reluctantly and disappear almost as quickly, leaving long nights that stretch on under a heavy darkness. The wind cuts through every layer of clothing, the snow packs hard over the fields, and the entire landscape appears frozen in complete stillness. Yet even in that frozen silence, work continues in ways that are less visible but no less important, as the soil rests and recovers, machinery is repaired in the shop, and plans for the coming season take shape.

I remember one winter when a cousin from Toronto came to visit and assumed we were far ahead of the times because every vehicle seemed to be electric, each one with a cord dangling from the front. The truth was far more practical than futuristic because those cords were for block heaters that kept the engines warm enough to start in the kind of cold that makes you think carefully before opening the door and stepping outside.

Spring arrives carrying a mixture of optimism and uncertainty as the work of planting begins and experiments are tried with no guarantees of success. Seeds go into the ground with the hope that the season will be kind, though no one can be certain what lies ahead. Summer follows with long days of tending, when growth is steady but slow and when the results of effort remain hidden beneath the surface. It is a season that demands patience and consistency, a willingness to keep going without the reassurance of immediate reward. Then comes fall, the time of harvest when the efforts of months are finally brought in, followed by reflection on what worked, what could be improved, and gratitude for what the year provided.

Every stage in this cycle matters, even the harshest and most unyielding stages, because growth is not a matter of constant forward motion but of moving through periods of planting, tending, resting, and renewal. The same rhythm holds true for our own development, where the seasons that feel the most dormant or even the most brutal often prepare us for the greatest periods of progress. Just as recessions in the economy clear away waste and inefficiency, the hard seasons of life strip out what is not essential and leave us leaner, sharper, and more focused on what matters most.

When you think back to one of the most difficult times you have faced and compare it to a period when life felt easy, the difference in the depth of growth becomes clear. The hard seasons are the ones that refine your skills, strengthen your resilience, and sharpen your sense of purpose. The easier seasons may be enjoyable, yet they rarely shape you with the same lasting impact.

The world will always offer an endless stream of invitations to play by its rules, urging you to rush so that you can deliver more, to overcompensate in order to please others, and to fill your time with activity so that you appear valuable. Your energy is finite, and your attention is a resource too precious to squander. You cannot win a game that has been designed to pull you away from your own values. The only way to measure your harvest is by how closely your actions align with the purpose that is yours alone.

This is why you must reclaim your definition of high value, remain within your circle of influence, say no as an act of integrity, allow your North Star to guide you, and continue planting seeds even in the darkest seasons, knowing that your future harvest depends on the quiet and purposeful work you choose to do when no one else is watching.

Project Pulse

When you play with your rules, then you own the field, and the officials, and the crowd. Don't forget that the home team wins far more often than the visitors.

References

Bezos, Jeff. 2016. *Amazon Shareholder Letter*.

Dyson, James. 1997. *Against the Odds: An Autobiography*. London: Orion.

Edmondson, Amy C. 2018. *The Fearless Organization: Creating Psychological Safety in the Workplace for Learning, Innovation, and Growth*. New Jersey: Wiley.

Kahneman, Daniel. 2011. *Thinking, Fast and Slow*. New York, NY: Farrar, Straus and Giroux.

Pink, Daniel H. 2005. *A Whole New Mind: Why Right-Brainers Will Rule the Future*. New York: Riverhead Books.

Project Management Institute. 2023. *Global Project Management Job Trends 2023 Report*. PMI.

Pfungst, Oskar. 1911. *Clever Hans: The Horse of Mr. von Osten*. New York: Henry Holt.

Robert, Michel, and Alan Weiss. 2000. *The Innovation Formula*. Provo, Utah: Executive Excellence Publishing.

Weiss, Alan. 2022. *Sentient Strategy: How to Create Market-Dominating Strategies in an Increasingly Unpredictable World*. New Jersey: Wiley.

About the Authors

Kursten Faller is a leadership and project management advisor with more than 25 years of experience helping organizations navigate complexity, change, and transformation. He holds a Bachelor of Applied Science in Industrial Systems Engineering from the University of Regina and a Master's Certificate in Project Management from the Schulich School of Business at York University. He is a licensed professional engineer and also holds international credentials, including Project Management Professional from the Project Management Institute and Brain Based Coach from the NeuroLeadership Institute.

His career has spanned leadership of projects in health care, oil and gas, utilities, mining, retail, manufacturing, agriculture, government, and education. After a decade in corporate consulting with a global multinational firm, he founded his own consultancy in 2012. Since then, he has worked with executives and teams across sectors, offering executive coaching, leadership development, and advisory services.

Kursten's perspective is shaped by experience as a client, consultant, vendor, subject matter expert, and project manager, giving him a rare understanding of projects from every angle. He has also lectured in project management at the University of Saskatchewan. This combination of academic credentials, professional achievements, and practical leadership across hundreds of projects uniquely prepares him to write on the intersection of leadership, psychology, and performance explored in this book.

Alan Weiss is a globally recognized consultant, speaker, and author, renowned for his expertise in organizational development and personal growth. As the founder of Summit Consulting Group, Inc., he has advised over 500 leading organizations worldwide, including Merck, Hewlett-Packard, GE, Mercedes-Benz, and the Federal Reserve.

With a PhD in psychology, Weiss has held academic positions at institutions such as the University of Rhode Island and has been a visiting faculty member at Case Western Reserve University, Boston College,

Tufts, and others. He is an inductee into the Professional Speaking Hall of Fame and a Fellow of the Institute of Management Consultants—one of only two individuals to hold both honors.

Weiss has authored over 60 books, including the best-selling *Million Dollar Consulting*, now in its sixth edition. His works have been translated into 15 languages and are used in curricula at institutions like Villanova, Temple University, and the Wharton School of Business. His latest book, *Your Legacy Is Now*, emphasizes the importance of creating meaning in one's life daily, rather than seeking it externally or deferring it to the future.

Residing in East Greenwich, Rhode Island, with his wife Maria, Weiss continues to influence professionals globally through his writing, speaking engagements, and consulting work.

Index

Note: Page numbers followed by f refers to figures.

www.ingramcontent.com/pod-product-compliance
Lightning Source LLC
Chambersburg PA
CBHW071013200526
45171CB00007B/120